North Carolina Local Government Contracting: Quick Reference and Related Statutes

2014

Norma R. Houston

UNC
SCHOOL OF
GOVERNMENT

The School of Government at the University of North Carolina at Chapel Hill works to improve the lives of North Carolinians by engaging in practical scholarship that helps public officials and citizens understand and improve state and local government. Established in 1931 as the Institute of Government, the School provides educational, advisory, and research services for state and local governments. The School of Government is also home to a nationally ranked graduate program in public administration and specialized centers focused on information technology and environmental finance.

As the largest university-based local government training, advisory, and research organization in the United States, the School of Government offers up to 200 courses, webinars, and specialized conferences for more than 12,000 public officials each year. In addition, faculty members annually publish approximately 50 books, manuals, reports, articles, bulletins, and other print and online content related to state and local government. Each day that the General Assembly is in session, the School produces the *Daily Bulletin Online*, which reports on the day's activities for members of the legislature and others who need to follow the course of legislation.

The Master of Public Administration Program is offered in two formats. The full-time, two-year residential program serves up to 60 students annually. In 2013 the School launched MPA@UNC, an online format designed for working professionals and others seeking flexibility while advancing their careers in public service. The School's MPA program consistently ranks among the best public administration graduate programs in the country, particularly in city management. With courses ranging from public policy analysis to ethics and management, the program educates leaders for local, state, and federal governments and nonprofit organizations.

Operating support for the School of Government's programs and activities comes from many sources, including state appropriations, local government membership dues, private contributions, publication sales, course fees, and service contracts. Visit www.sog.unc.edu or call 919.966.5381 for more information on the School's courses, publications, programs, and services.

Michael R. Smith, Dean
Thomas H. Thornburg, Senior Associate Dean
Frayda S. Bluestein, Associate Dean for Faculty Development
L. Ellen Bradley, Associate Dean for Programs and Marketing
Johnny Burleson, Associate Dean for Development
Todd A. Nicolet, Associate Dean for Operations
Bradley G. Volk, Associate Dean for Administration

FACULTY

Whitney Afonso	Richard D. Ducker	Christopher B. McLaughlin	Jessica Smith
Trey Allen	Joseph S. Ferrell	Kara A. Millonzi	Meredith Smith
Gregory S. Allison	Alyson A. Grine	Jill D. Moore	Carl W. Stenberg III
David N. Ammons	Norma Houston	Jonathan Q. Morgan	John B. Stephens
Ann M. Anderson	Cheryl Daniels Howell	Ricardo S. Morse	Charles Szypszak
Maureen Berner	Jeffrey A. Hughes	C. Tyler Mulligan	Shannon H. Tufts
Mark F. Botts	Willow S. Jacobson	Kimberly L. Nelson	Vaughn Mamlin Upshaw
Michael Crowell	Robert P. Joyce	David W. Owens	Aimee N. Wall
Leisha DeHart-Davis	Diane M. Juffras	LaToya B. Powell	Jeffrey B. Welty
Shea Riggsbee Denning	Dona G. Lewandowski	William C. Rivenbark	Richard B. Whisnant
Sara DePasquale	Adam Lovelady	Dale J. Roenigk	
James C. Drennan	James M. Markham	John Rubin	

© 2014
School of Government
The University of North Carolina at Chapel Hill

Printed in the United States of America

21 20 19 18 17   3 4 5 6 7

ISBN 978-1-56011-756-8

♻ This publication is printed on permanent, acid-free paper in compliance with the North Carolina General Statutes.

Contents

Part I

Overview of Local Government Contracting, Bidding, and Property Disposal Requirements   1

CHAPTER 5
Conflicts of Interest and Other Limitations　29

CHAPTER 6
Property Disposal   35

CHAPTER 7
Related Statutory Provisions   41

Part II
Selected General Statutes   49

E. Related Statutory Provisions   137

Preface

This quick reference for the contracting, bidding, and property disposal requirements applicable to North Carolina local governments is organized in two parts and is designed to provide general guidance to public officials and others interested in the public contracting process. Part I of the book contains an overview of local government contracting, bidding, and property disposal requirements, while selected North Carolina General Statutes governing contracting and bidding are included in Part II. Parenthetical citations in the text beside primary headings in Part I refer to the relevant sections of the North Carolina General Statutes (G.S.).

This publication is a revision of two guides previously published by the Institute/School of Government, *An Overview of Contract Bidding Requirements for North Carolina Local Governments* by Frayda S. Bluestein and *An Outline of Statutory Provisions Controlling Purchasing by Local Governments in North Carolina* by Warren Jake Wicker. Wicker first conceived of and created this guide in 1959. It is a tribute to his dedication to public officials that the original work was updated eighteen times between 1959 and 1996. Bluestein's updates between 1996 and 2007 faithfully carried this dedication forward to the present. This edition is dedicated to both Jake Wicker and Frayda Bluestein with the hope that it will maintain both the quality and the brevity exemplified by their earlier work.

The current and all previous editions of this publication would not be possible without the unflagging dedication, competence, and patience of the School of Government Publications Division. Special thanks to Melissa Twomey, Dan Soileau, and Lisa Wright for their efforts in bringing this current edition to fruition.

Introduction

As the title suggests, this publication is a quick reference. It is intended to give readers a general introduction to the statutory procedures that govern contracting, procurement, and property disposal by local government agencies and to serve as a "roadmap" through those procedures. It does not provide exhaustive or detailed explanations. For more information, consult Part II of the text, which includes many of the statutes cited in Part I, as well as the following School of Government publications:

Bluestein, Frayda S. *A Legal Guide to Purchasing and Contracting for North Carolina Local Governments.* 2nd ed. Chapel Hill, NC: UNC School of Government, 2004 (see also 2007 supplement).

Houston, Norma R., and Jessica Jansepar Ross. "HUB Participation in Building Construction Contracting by N.C. Local Governments: Statutory Requirements and Constitutional Limitations." *Local Government Law Bulletin* No. 131 (Feb. 2013).

Bell, A. Fleming, II. *Ethics, Conflicts, and Offices: A Guide for Local Officials.* 2nd ed. Chapel Hill, NC: UNC School of Government, 2011.

Millonzi, Kara A. *Introduction to Local Government Finance,* 2nd ed. Chapel Hill, NC: UNC School of Government, 2014.

———. *Local Government Budget and Fiscal Control Act.* 7th ed. Chapel Hill, NC: UNC School of Government, 2011.

Lawrence, David M. *Local Government Property Transactions in North Carolina.* 7th ed. Chapel Hill, NC: UNC School of Government, 2000.

A number of bulletins, legislative updates, and other publications on issues affecting public purchasing, contracting, and property disposal are available through the School of Government's Publications Sales Office (919.966.4119) or online at www.sog.unc.edu. Also, numerous posts on the School's *Coates' Canons: NC Local Government Law Blog* address purchasing, contracting, property disposal, and finance legal issues (http://canons.sog.unc.edu/). Finally, the School's Local Government Purchasing and Contracting website contains a variety of useful tools, sample forms, and other reference materials (www.ncpurchasing.unc.edu).

PART I

Overview of Local Government Contracting, Bidding, and Property Disposal Requirements

CHAPTER 1

Coverage and Applicability of Bidding Requirements

A. Types of Local Governments Covered

The main competitive bidding requirements for local governments are contained in Article 8 of Chapter 143 of the North Carolina General Statutes (hereinafter G.S.). Most of the formal bidding requirements are set forth in G.S. 143-129, and the informal requirements can be found in G.S. 143-131. These statutes apply to the "expenditure of public money" within established dollar limits and on certain types of contracts (described below). The statutes do not identify the specific entities covered. Therefore, unless a specific statute provides otherwise, these bidding requirements apply to all local government entities, including municipalities, counties, local school units, special districts, and other special purpose local governments.

Several types of local governments are either exempt from bidding requirements or are subject to laws that establish special contracting procedures. These local governments include hospital authorities,[1] housing authorities,[2] regional solid waste management authorities,[3] soil and water conservation districts,[4] joint municipal power agencies,[5] and transportation authorities.[6]

---

1. Section 131E-23(d) of the North Carolina General Statutes (hereinafter G.S.).
2. G.S. 157-9(a).
3. G.S. 153A-427(b).
4. G.S. 131E-23(d).
5. G.S. 159B-11(10).
6. G.S. 143-129(h).

Community colleges, although considered local governments for some purposes, are subject to different rules for certain types of contracts under separate specific statutory provisions. For example, community colleges are required to purchase all supplies, materials, and equipment in accordance with "contracts made by or with the approval of the Purchase and Contract Division of the Department of Administration."[7] The main procedures that govern these contracts (and the contracts of most state agencies) are found in Article 3 of G.S. Chapter 143 and in the policies and regulations of the Department of Administration, Division of Purchase and Contract. These rules generally require community colleges to purchase from sources to which statewide contracts have been awarded (commonly known as *state contract vendors*). They also generally require the use of state policies and state approval for bidding purchases. Flexibility to purchase from other sources is provided in limited circumstances under G.S. 115D-58.14. For construction or repair contracts, community colleges are subject to the same procedures as other local governments. Most of these procedures are found in Article 8 of G.S. Chapter 143. When contracting for architectural, engineering, or surveying services or for alternative construction delivery methods (discussed in chapter 4) community colleges, like local governments generally, are required to use the qualifications-based selection procedures provided for in G.S. 143-64.31 (sometimes referred to as the *Mini-Brooks Act*).

B. Types of Contracts Covered

Statutory bidding requirements generally apply to two categories of contracts:

(1) Contracts for the purchase of apparatus, supplies, materials, or equipment
(2) Contracts for construction or repair work

The first category is generally understood to include all types of personal property. The second category is generally understood to include both horizontal construction (roads, utilities, water and sewer lines, and other infra-

---

7. G.S. 115D-58.5(b).

structure) and vertical construction (buildings, elevated water tanks, and other structures). Special rules apply to building construction projects.

Contracts that are not subject to competitive bidding requirements because they do not fall within either of the two categories listed above include

(1) service contracts (but note the special rules for contracts with architects, engineers, and surveyors and for contracts involving alternative construction delivery methods discussed in chapter 4, sections D and H);

(2) contracts for the purchase of real property; and

(3) contracts for the lease of personal property (but note that lease-purchase or lease contracts with an option to purchase are subject to bidding.[8]

Contracts that fall below the informal bidding threshold (see chapter 3) also are not subject to any statutory procedural requirements, although they may be subject to competitive bidding requirements imposed by local policy.

Many local governments have policies that require them to conduct bidding procedures for contracts that are not subject to statutory bidding requirements, and some may do so on a case-by-case basis by local discretion. In these situations, the local unit is not required to use the statutory procedures, but it may opt to use some or all of them or may develop procedures of its own, provided those procedures are not in conflict with state law. While establishment of local procedures is not legally mandated, failure to comply with established local procedures may invalidate the resulting contract.

---

8. G.S. 160A-19; 153A-165.

CHAPTER 2

Formal Bidding Requirements (G.S. 143-129)

A. Coverage

The formal bidding requirements cover construction or repair contracts estimated to cost $500,000 or more and the purchase of apparatus, supplies, materials, or equipment (hereinafter purchase contracts) estimated to cost $90,000 or more. The threshold applies to the estimated cost of the total contract, not to each item. The bidding requirements also apply to lease-purchase contracts and leases containing an option to purchase.[1] By law, contracts shall not be divided for the purpose of evading the bidding requirements.[2]

B. Advertising for Bids (G.S. 143-129)

1. Where?

Bidding opportunities must be advertised in a newspaper having "general circulation" (defined in Section 1-597 of the North Carolina General Statutes (hereinafter G.S.)) in the jurisdiction that is seeking bids. Notice of bidding opportunities may be provided in other ways, e.g., by electronic means such

---

1. Sections 160A-19, 153A-165 of the North Carolina General Statutes (hereinafter G.S.).

2. G.S. 143-133.

as website posting, in addition to by published notice. Advertising by electronic means only requires governing board approval at a regular meeting.[3]

2. When?

The advertisement must appear at least one time and at least seven full days must lapse between the date on which the advertisement appears and the date of the opening of bids.[4]

3. What?

The advertisement must state the time and place where interested parties may obtain plans and specifications, specify the time and place for opening the bids, and reserve to the governing body the right to reject any or all bids.[5]

C. Receipt and Opening of Bids; Form; Number of Bids (G.S. 143-129, -129.9, -132; 132-1, -1.2)

1. Public Opening

All proposals must be opened in public.[6]

2. Sealed Bid

Bids must be submitted sealed and cannot be opened prior to the advertised date and time of the bid opening. Knowingly opening a sealed bid or disclosing the contents of a bid without the permission of the bidder prior to the bid opening is a Class 1 misdemeanor.[7]

3. Form

Bids for purchase contracts may be received either in paper form or electronically; bids for construction or repair projects must be received in paper form. Procedures for receiving purchase bids electronically must be designed "to ensure the security, authenticity, and confidentiality of the bids to at least the same extent as is provided for with sealed paper bids."[8]

---

3. G.S. 143-129(b).
4. *Id.*
5. *Id.*
6. *Id.*
7. *Id.*
8. G.S. 143-129.9(a)(2).

4. Minimum Number

A minimum of three bids are required *only for construction or repair contracts in the formal bidding range.* If three bids are not received, the unit must reject the bids received and readvertise; if three bids are not received after the second advertisement, the unit may open the bids and award the contract.[9] No minimum number of bids is required for purchase contracts.

5. Public Records

By operation of the public records law, formal bids are subject to public inspection once they are opened.[10] Trade secrets contained in bids are not public if properly identified at the time the bid is submitted.[11]

D. Reverse Auctions (G.S. 143-129, -129.9)

Local governments are authorized to use *reverse auctions* for purchase contracts as an alternative to the sealed bid procedure.[12] A reverse auction is "a real-time purchasing process in which bidders compete to provide goods at the lowest selling price in an open and interactive environment."[13] Bidders' prices may be revealed during the reverse auction. A local government may conduct reverse auctions independently, through the state electronic procurement system, or through a third party under contract with the local government.[14]

The requirements for advertising bidding opportunities, timeliness of the receipt of bids, the standard for the award of contracts, and other aspects of the bidding laws apply to reverse auctions to the extent they are not inconsistent with the reverse auction process.[15] The law prohibits the use of reverse auctions for the purchase of construction aggregates (crushed stone, sand, gravel, etc.).[16]

---

9. G.S. 143-132(a).
10. G.S. 132-1.
11. G.S. 132-1.2.
12. G.S. 143-129.
13. G.S. 143-129.9(a)(1).
14. *Id.*
15. G.S. 143-129.9(b).
16. G.S. 143-129.9(c).

E. Bid Deposit or Bond (G.S. 143-129)

Bids for construction or repair work in the formal bidding range must be accompanied by a bond or deposit equal to at least 5 percent of the amount of the bid. Bid bonds/deposits are not required for any purchase contracts or for construction or repair contracts in the informal bidding range.

A formal construction bid that is not accompanied by a bid bond/deposit at the time the bid is submitted cannot be considered or accepted and thus cannot be counted toward the three-bid minimum required to open bids. The bid deposit may be in any of the following forms: cash, cashier's check, certified check, or bid bond executed by a surety licensed in North Carolina. If the successful bidder does not execute the contract within ten days after the contract is awarded or fails to give satisfactory surety as required by law, the bidder forfeits the bid bond/deposit.[17]

F. Evaluating Bids; Negotiations When Bids Exceed Funds Available (G.S. 143-129, -129.1, -129.9)

1. Responsive Bid

Bids must be *responsive*, which means that they comply with all applicable laws and substantially meet the requirements of the specifications. While a local government may not waive a defect in legal requirements, it may waive minor deviations (variations) from its specifications. However, it is legally prohibited from waiving variations that are *material*. A material variation is one that, if waived, would give the bidder "an advantage or benefit which is not enjoyed by other bidders."[18] A bid that does not comply with all applicable legal requirements or that contains a material variation must be rejected as nonresponsive.

2. Negotiations

Units may negotiate with bidders after bids are opened only in one instance. If all bid prices exceed funds available for the project or purchase, the unit may enter into negotiations with the lowest responsive, responsible bid-

---

17. G.S. 143-129.9(b).

18. Prof'l Food Servs. Mgmt., Inc. v. N.C. Dep't of Admin., 109 N.C. App. 265, 269 (1993) (internal quotation marks, citations omitted).

der making reasonable changes to the plans or specifications necessary to bring the contract price to within funds available if the bidder agrees to the changes. The unitmay then award the contract to that bidder.[19]

G. Withdrawal of Bid Because of Error (G.S. 143-129.1)

Under G.S. 143-129.1, a bidder may request permission to withdraw his or her bid after the bid opening if the bidder can submit credible evidence that the bid was based on a mistake that constituted a substantial "unintentional arithmetic error or unintentional omission"—but not a judgment error—in the preparation of the bid. The request to withdraw must be made in writing no later than seventy-two hours after the opening of bids, unless a longer period has been specified in the instructions to bidders. If the agency determines that the error meets the standard under the statute, the bid may be withdrawn. If not, the bidder forfeits his or her bid bond/deposit. A bidder who requests withdrawal cannot participate in the contract, even on readvertisement.

H. Standards and Procedures for Awarding the Contract (G.S. 143-129)

1. Responsible Bidder

The contract award shall be made to the "lowest responsible bidder, or bidders, taking into consideration quality, performance and the time specified in the proposals for the performance of the contract."[20] The term "responsible" has been interpreted to imply "skill, judgment and integrity necessary to the faithful performance of the contract, as well as sufficient financial resources and ability."[21] The successful bid also must be responsive, meaning that it must comply with all applicable legal requirements and substantially conform to the unit's specifications (see the discussion in section F, above).

---

19. G.S. 143-129.9(b).

20. G.S. 143-129(b).

21. Kinsey Contracting Co. v. City of Fayetteville, 106 N.C. App. 383, 385 (internal quotation marks, citations omitted), *discretionary review denied*, 332 N.C. 345 (1992).

2. Award

Contracts for purchases and for construction or repair work in the formal bidding range must be awarded by the governing body.[22] The governing body may delegate to the manager or purchasing agent, or both, the authority to award purchase contracts in the formal range, but it may not delegate such authority regarding contracts for construction or repair work.[23]

I. Contract Execution; Performance and Payment Bonds (G.S. 143-129)

1. Execution

All contracts that are subject to the formal bidding requirements must be executed in writing.[24] There are no statutory provisions specifying who must execute the contract, so the unit may authorize the official or employee of its choosing.

2. Performance and Payment Bonds

Where the sum of all contracts for a construction or repair project exceeds $300,000, the successful bidder must provide performance and payment bonds for the full amount of each contract exceeding $50,000.[25] In place of bonds, the contractor may provide cash, certified checks, or government securities.[26]

J. Exceptions to Competitive Bidding Requirements

Some of the exceptions listed below apply only to purchase contracts, some apply only to construction or repair contracts, and some apply to both purchase and construction or repair contracts. As noted previously (see chapter 1, section A), community colleges are subject to state rules for purchase contracts, so the exceptions in this section that apply to purchase contracts

---

22. G.S. 143-129(b).
23. G.S. 143-129(a).
24. G.S. 143-129(c).
25. G.S. 143-129(c); 44A-26.
26. G.S. 143-129(c).

do not apply to community colleges. Exceptions to the bidding requirements for community colleges can be found in the procedures and policies of the Department of Administration, Division of Purchase and Contract.

Except as otherwise noted, the exceptions listed below apply to contracts in both the formal and informal bidding ranges.

(1) Exceptions that apply to **purchase contracts only**:
   (a) *Purchases directly from other governmental agencies.*[27] Purchases made from agencies of the federal government, any state, and local governments in this or any other state, including purchases from government electronic bidding sites.
   (b) *Competitive group purchasing programs.*[28] Purchases made through a formally organized group purchasing program that offers competitively bid items at discount prices to two or more public agencies.
   (c) *Purchases of gasoline, diesel fuel, alcohol fuel, motor oil, fuel oil, or natural gas.*[29] Although exempt from formal bidding requirements, informal bidding is required for any fuel purchase costing $30,000 or more.
   (d) *Sole source purchases.*[30] A contract under this exception requires governing board approval and applies only if performance or price competition for a product is not available, a needed product is available from only one source of supply, or standardization or compatibility is the overriding consideration. Separate provisions for soles sources apply to hospitals under this exception.
   (e) *Information technology.* Information technology goods or services purchased directly through state Office of Information Technology[31] or under an optional request for proposals (RFP) procedure.[32]

---

27. G.S. 143-129(e)(1).
28. G.S. 143-129(e)(3).
29. G.S. 143-129(e)(5).
30. G.S. 143-129(e)(6).
31. G.S. 143-129(e)(7).
32. G.S. 143-129.8.

(f) *State contract purchases.*[33] Purchases from vendors under contract with a North Carolina state agency, so long as the vendor is willing to sell the same item under the same or more favorable prices, terms, and conditions as under the state contract.

(g) *Federal contract purchases.*[34] Purchases from vendors under contract with a federal agency, so long as the vendor is willing to sell the same item under the same or more favorable prices, terms, and conditions as under the federal contract.

(h) *Used items.*[35] Purchases of used apparatus, supplies, materials, or equipment. This exception does not include remanufactured, refabricated, or demo items.

(i) *Previously bid or "piggybacking" contracts.*[36] A contract under this exception requires governing board approval at a regular meeting upon ten days public notice, and the original contract must have been entered into within the previous twelve months using competitive bidding procedures. This exception is only available for purchase contracts in the formal bidding range.

(j) *Purchases of goods and services from nonprofit work centers for the blind and severely disabled.* An eligible nonprofit work center must meet the definition of such an entity under G.S. 143-48.[37]

(k) *Public school food service products.*[38] This exception is available for purchases by public schools of food products and services for school food and nutrition services programs.

(l) *Public school books.*[39] This exception is available for purchases by public schools of published books, manuscripts, maps, pamphlets, and periodicals.

---

33. G.S. 143-129(e)(9).
34. G.S. 143-129(e)(9a).
35. G.S. 143-129(e)(10).
36. G.S. 143-129(g).
37. G.S. 143-129.5.
38. G.S. 115C-264.
39. G.S. 115C-522(a).

(m) *Voting systems.*[40] Purchases by counties of voting systems certified by the State Board of Elections.

(2) Exceptions that apply to **construction or repair contracts only**:

(a) *Change order work.*[41] The term *change order work* is defined in G.S. 143-129 as "[c]onstruction or repair work undertaken during the progress of a construction or repair project initially begun pursuant to this section."

(b) *Construction management at risk projects.*[42] These contracts are governed by G.S. 143-128.1. (See Chapter 4, Section H for discussion of this and other alternative construction delivery methods.)

(c) *Force account work* (see Chapter 4, Section G).[43] This entails work performed by full-time employees of the government unit where the total cost of the project does not exceed $125,000 or the total cost of the labor does not exceed $50,000. Competitive bidding requirements apply to materials purchased for these kinds of projects, and governing board approval of the work is required.

(d) *Projects using unemployment-relief labor.*[44] This exception applies whether the labor is paid for in whole or in part with state or federal funds.

(e) *DOT contracts.*[45] Contracts entered into by a municipality with the North Carolina Department of Transportation (DOT) for street construction and repair of municipal streets.

(3) Exceptions that apply to **both construction and purchase contracts**:

(a) *Emergencies.*[46] Special emergency cases involving an imminent or actual threat to the health and safety of the people or their property.

---

40. G.S. 163-165.8.
41. G.S. 143-129(e)(4).
42. G.S. 143-129(e)(11).
43. G.S. 143-135.
44. G.S. 143-129(d).
45. G.S. 136-41.3
46. G.S. 143-129(e)(2).

(b) *Guaranteed energy savings contracts.*[47] These contracts are subject to the requirements of G.S. 143-64.17 through -64.17G.

(c) *Solid waste management facilities.*[48] The construction and operation of solid waste management facilities may be contracted for under an optional request for proposals (RFP) procedure.

---

47. G.S. 143-129(e)(8).
48. G.S. 143-129.2.

CHAPTER 3

Informal Bidding Requirements (G.S. 143-131)

A. Coverage

Informal bidding requirements apply to contracts for construction or repair work and to contracts for the purchase or lease-purchase of apparatus, supplies, materials, or equipment involving the expenditure of $30,000 or more up to the limits prescribed by the formal bidding requirements ($500,000 for construction; $90,000 for purchase).[1] As with formal bids, the threshold applies to the total contract, not to each item, and contracts cannot be divided for the purpose of evading the bidding requirements.[2]

B. Procedures (G.S. 143-131)

Informal bids must be secured. There are no specific requirements for the solicitation or form of bids. They may be solicited and obtained verbally or by electronic or written submission. No advertisement is required. No minimum number of bids is required. Requirements for soliciting minority participation for certain building projects in the informal range are noted in chapter 4, section B. The unit must keep a record of all bids submitted, and this record is not subject to public inspection until the contract has been awarded.[3]

---

1. Section 143-131(a) of the North Carolina General Statutes (hereinafter G.S.).
2. G.S. 143-133.
3. G.S. 143-131.

C. Standard for Awarding the Contract (G.S. 143-131)

As with formal bids, informal contracts must be awarded to the "lowest responsible, responsive bidder, taking into consideration quality, performance, and the time specified in the bids for the performance of the contract."[4] The term "responsible" has been interpreted to imply "skill, judgment and integrity necessary to the faithful performance of the contract, as well as sufficient financial resources and ability."[5]

---

4. G.S. 143-131(a).

5. Kinsey Contracting Co. v. City of Fayetteville, 106 N.C. App. 383, 385 (internal quotation marks, citations omitted), *discretionary review denied*, 332 N.C. 345, 421 S.E.2d 149 (1992).

CHAPTER 4

Additional Requirements for Construction Contracts

As noted in chapter 2, several of the requirements in the formal bidding statutes apply only to construction or repair contracts in the formal range. These include the following requirements:

(1) A bid bond/deposit of at least 5 percent of the bid amount must be submitted with the bid

(2) Performance and payment bonds must be supplied by the successful bidder on contracts costing $50,000 or more on projects costing a total of $300,000 or more)

(3) A minimum of three bids must be received in order to open bids (note that a bid which does not include a bid bond/deposit cannot be counted toward the three-bid minimum requirement)

(4) Contracts must be awarded by the governing board.

This chapter discusses additional statutory requirements that apply only to construction or repair projects.

A. Building Construction Projects over $300,000 (G.S. 143-128)

The requirements identified in this section apply to construction or repair projects involving a building estimated to cost more than $300,000. These requirements do not apply if the project does not involve a building, but instead involves work such as street paving, utility line installation, or elevated water tank repairs.

1. Construction Bidding Methods That May Be Used

The following methods for bidding are permitted under G.S. 143-128(a1):

(1) Separate-prime bidding under Section 143-128(b) of the North Carolina General Statutes (hereinafter G.S.)

(2) Single-prime bidding under G.S. 143-128(d)

(3) Dual bidding (separate- and single-prime) under G.S. 143-128(d1)

(4) Construction management at risk under G.S. 143-128.1

(5) Design-build under G.S. 143-128.1A

(6) Design-build bridging under G.S. 143-128.1B

(7) Public-private partnership contracts under G.S. 143-128.1C.

(8) Alternative method authorized by the State Building Commission under G.S. 143-135.26(9)

2. Historically Underutilized Business (HUB) Participation Goals

a. HUB Definition

"Historically underutilized business" is defined by statute and includes businesses owned by ethnic minorities, women, and socially and economically disadvantaged individuals.[1]

b. Goal Number

A verifiable goal for HUB participation is required for local projects. The state goal of 10 percent is to be used for projects of $100,000 or more involving state appropriated or grant funds, unless a preexisting local goal is justified.[2]

c. Good Faith Requirement

Good faith efforts to encourage participation by HUBs in public projects must be made by the public agency[3] and by the bidders on a given project.[4] The failure of a bidder to comply with these requirements is grounds for rejection of the bid.[5]

---

1. Sections 143-128.4(a) and (b) of the North Carolina General Statutes (hereinafter G.S.).
2. G.S. 143-128.2(a)
3. G.S. 143-128.2(b), (e).
4. G.S. 143-128.2(f).
5. G.S. 143-128.2(c).

d. *Reports; Documentation; Certification*

Agencies must comply with reporting requirements established by the State Department of Administration and must document good faith efforts made and participation obtained for each project. HUBs must be certified with the Department of Administration's Office for Historically Underutilized Businesses in order to count toward the agency's participation goals.[6]

3. Dispute Resolution Requirements

Dispute resolution procedures must be provided for all building construction projects, regardless of the dollar value (the procedures may establish a minimum amount in controversy of $15,000). Local governments may adopt procedures established by the State Building Commission or may establish their own. Procedures must provide the option of using mediation and must be available for all parties involved in the project, including the architect, the contractors, and subcontractors at all levels.[7]

B. Building Construction Projects between $30,000 and $300,000

1. Historically Underutilized Business (HUB) Participation Efforts and Reporting (G.S. 143-131(b); see generally G.S. 143-128.2)

Public agencies are required to solicit participation by HUBs and to maintain a record of contractors solicited and efforts made to recruit HUB participation. Advertisement for bids is not required.

Agencies must comply with reporting requirements established by the State Department of Administration and must document efforts made and HUB participation obtained for each project.[8]

2. Dispute Resolution Requirements

The same requirements applicable to building construction projects over $300,000 apply to projects between $30,000 and $300,000 (see section A.3, above).

---

6. G.S. 143-128.3.

7. G.S. 143-128(f1).

8. G.S. 143-131(b).

C. Contractor Licensing (G.S. Chapter 87, Article 1)

Contractors on construction or repair projects must comply with state contractor licensing requirements. The contract threshold for licensure of general contractors is $30,000.[9] Licenses are not required for work performed by the unit's own forces (see section G, below). Architects and engineers who prepare specifications for public projects are required to include information about licensure requirements in the invitation to bidders and in the specifications.[10] If the project requires licensure, the contract cannot be awarded to an unlicensed contractor.

D. Use and Selection of Design Professionals (G.S. 133-1.1; see generally G.S. Chapter 143, Article 3D)

1. Use of Design Professionals

Plans and specifications for public building construction or repair projects must be prepared by a registered architect or a registered engineer (or both, depending upon the requirements of the project) when the expenditure exceeds

(1) $300,000 for projects that do not include "major structural change in framing or foundation support systems;"
(2) $100,000 for the repair of public buildings "affecting life safety systems;"
(3) $135,000, for projects that include "major structural change in framing or foundation support systems;" or
(4) $135,000, for the construction of, or additions to, public buildings.[11]

2. Selection of Design Professionals

a. Announcement; Selection; Price

Requirements for architectural, engineering, and surveying services must be "announced," and firms must be selected based on "demonstrated competence and qualification . . . without regard to fee other than unit price

---

9. G.S. 87-1.
10. G.S. 87-15.
11. G.S. 133-1.1(a).

information . . ."[12] Contract price cannot be solicited or provided during the request for qualifications (RFQ) process. Contract price can only be negotiated after the unit has evaluated proposals and determined which firm is the best qualified. If negotiations with the best qualified firm are not successful, the unit may proceed to negotiate contract price with the second-best qualified firm, and so on.[13]

Local governments are prohibited from requiring firms to generate work product (such as preliminary drawings) as part of the RFQ process. Examples of prior completed work on other projects may be solicited.[14]

b. Good Faith Requirement

Good faith efforts must be used to notify minority firms of the opportunity to submit qualifications for consideration by the public entity.

c. Exemption—Contracts Involving Professional Fees under $50,000

Local governments may "in writing exempt particular projects" from the qualification-based selection requirement for contracts with an estimated professional fee of less than $50,000. The exemption cannot be used for contracts where the estimated professional fee is $50,000 or greater.[15]

d. Exemption—Community College Projects under $500,000

Community college capital improvement projects costing less than $500,000 are exempt from the qualifications-based selection requirement.[16]

E. Competitive Specifications Required (G.S. 133-3)

Under G.S. 133-3, specifications for materials to be used in public construction projects shall specify performance and design characteristics. When this is impossible, brand name specifications may be used, but three or more examples of equivalent design must be listed and specifications must indicate that the examples are used to denote the standards required and are not restrictive. If three examples are not available, specifications

---

12. G.S. 143-64.31(a).
13. *Id.*
14. *Id.*
15. G.S. 143-64.32.
16. G.S. 143-64.34.

must list as many examples as are available. Specifications may list one or more preferred brands in limited circumstances, subject to requirements for justification and approval set forth in the statute, including approval by the public owner at an open meeting. Substitutions shall be submitted to the designer for approval or disapproval, which must be made prior to the opening of bids.

F. Plans Approved by State Department of Insurance (G.S. 58-31-40)

Under G.S. 58-31-40, county, city, or school district plans and specifications for construction of a building comprising 20,000 square feet or more must be approved by the Department of Insurance as to fire safety.

G. Use of Force Account Labor; Limitations (G.S. 143-135)

Local governments may use their own forces (employees) on construction and repair projects where the total cost of the project is less than $125,000 or the total cost of the labor is less than $50,000. The work must be performed by employees on the permanent payroll and must be approved by the governing board.[17]

If the cost of the project is more than $30,000, the local government must submit an owner-contractor affidavit to the local building inspector attesting to its eligibility to act as its own general contractor in lieu of hiring a licensed general contractor to supervise the project.[18]

Purchases of apparatus, supplies, materials, or equipment for use in force account work must comply with the normal bidding requirements. Construction or repair work shall not be divided for the purposes of evading competitive bidding requirements.[19]

---

17. G.S. 143-135.
18. G.S. 87-14.
19. G.S. 143-133.

H. Alternative Construction Delivery Methods (G.S. 143-64.31, -128 through -128.1C, -135.26)

1. Construction Management at Risk

Under this method, the construction manager at risk, who must be a licensed general contractor, provides construction management services and guarantees the total cost of the project. The construction manager at risk acts as the fiduciary of the local government in handling and opening bids and in awarding contracts. Plans and specifications must be drawn by a licensed architect or engineer who contracts directly with the local government. The construction manager at risk must be selected based on qualifications, not estimated costs of the contract; contract costs can only be negotiated after the best qualified construction manager is initially selected.[20]

2. Design-Build

The design-builder contracts to provide both design services (architectural and engineering) and construction services under one contract. A design-build contract is subject to a specific statutory RFQ (request for qualifications) process, and the design-builder is initially selected based on qualifications, not on estimated costs of the contract. Contract costs can only be negotiated after the best qualified design-builder is initially selected.[21]

3. Design-Build Bridging

With this method, the unit of government contracts separately with a project designer to design 35 percent of the project, and then contracts with a design-builder to complete project design and perform construction services. The preliminary project designer is selected based on qualifications, while the design-build contract is awarded to the lowest responsive, responsible bidder based on estimated costs of performing general contract conditions, design services, and construction services.[22]

---

20. *See* G.S. 143-128.1, -64.31.
21. *See* G.S. 143-128.1A, -64.31.
22. *See* G.S. 143-128.1B, -64.31.

4. Public-Private Partnership

The unit of government contracts with a private developer to jointly develop a capital construction project under this method. The developer is selected based on qualifications through a competitive RFQ process and is required to finance at least 50 percent of the project cost.[23]

5. Other Alternative Methods

Other alternative construction methods are only allowed for building construction and repair projects costing $300,000 or more if approved by the State Building Commission or by legislative action. Alternative construction methods can be used without special approval for building construction and repair projects costing less than $300,000 as well as for all non-building construction and repair projects regardless of cost.[24]

6. Reporting

Local governments are required to report their use of alternative construction delivery methods to the N.C. Department of Administration. The report must include an explanation of why the particular alternative delivery method was used in lieu of a traditional method. Failure to file the report within twelve months of project completion may result in the local government being prohibited from using an alternative method on any projects until the report is submitted.[25]

I. Payment to Construction Contractors/ Retainage (G.S. 143-134.1)

Under G.S. 143-134.1, public owners may not withhold payment due to contractors (retainage) on construction or repair projects costing less than $100,000. For projects costing $100,000 or more, retainage is limited to no more than 5 percent of the periodic payment due, and retainage after the project is 50 percent complete is prohibited. When a certificate of substantial completion is issued, the public owner may retain up to 2.5 percent of the value of the remaining work to ensure final completion and correction of

---

23. *See* G.S. 143-128.1C, -64.31.
24. *See* G.S. 143-128(a1)(5), -135.26(9).
25. G.S. 143-133.1.

defective work. Regardless of the cost of the project, retainage is allowed in specified circumstances, such as when there is unsatisfactory job progress or defective work that has not been remedied.

J. Prequalification (G.S. 143-135.8)

Local governments may prequalify potential bidders on construction and repair projects. In doing so, a local government must adopt (1) an objective prequalification criteria policy applicable to all projects for which the unit chooses to use prequalification and (2) the specific assessment tool to be used in prequalifying bidders for a particular project. While the policy must be approved by the governing board, the assessment tool may be adopted by staff without board approval and may be modified on a project-by-project basis.

The prequalification policy must, among other requirements, establish a process by which a contractor who has been denied prequalification may protest that denial. If such a protest is successful, that contractor's bid must be accepted.

Bids submitted by bidders who were not prequalified must be rejected as nonresponsive.

The local government's prequalification policy must be used by a construction manager at risk when prequalifying first-tier subcontractors, as required under G.S. 143-128.1.

Prequalification may be used only on construction contracts bid using the single-prime, separate-prime, and dual bidding methods. Prequalification is specifically prohibited when contracting for design services (architectural, engineering, or surveying) or for alternative construction delivery methods (design-build, design-build bridging, and public-private partnerships) under the qualifications-based selection method required by G.S. Chapter 143, Article 3D (see section D of this chapter).

CHAPTER 5

Conflicts of Interest and Other Limitations

A. Public Officers or Employees Benefiting from Contracts (G.S. 14-234)

1. Prohibition

State law prohibits public officers and employees from

(1) deriving a *direct benefit* (see the section immediately below for a definition of this term) from contracts they are involved in making or administering;[1]

(2) attempting to influence any other person who is responsible for making or administering a contract from which the public officer or employee derives a direct benefit;[2] or

(3) soliciting or receiving any gift, reward, or promise of reward in exchange for recommending, influencing, or attempting to influence the award of a contract by the public agency.[3]

2. Direct Benefit

For purposes of the conflict of interest limitation pertaining to contracts (see the section immediately above), a person derives a direct benefit if the person or his or her spouse

(1) has more than a 10 percent interest in the entity that is a party to the contract;

---

1. Section 14-234(a)(1) of the North Carolina General Statutes (hereinafter G.S.).
2. G.S. 14-234(a)(2).
3. G.S. 14-234(a)(3).

(2) derives any income or commission directly from the contract; or

(3) acquires property under the contract.[4]

3. Exceptions

There are exceptions to the statutory prohibition against directly benefiting from a public contract. These include situations involving the following:

(1) Contracts with banks and utilities[5]

(2) Property conveyed under a court order in a condemnation proceeding[6]

(3) Employment contracts with the spouses of public officers[7]

(4) Remuneration for goods or services provided under public assistance programs, subject to certain conditions[8]

Also, contracts with public officers—including city, county, and school governing board members and appointed members of specified boards—are authorized for any municipality with a population of no more than 15,000 and for any county or school jurisdiction with no incorporated municipality of more than 15,000. Such contracts may not exceed, within a twelve-month period, $20,000 for medically-related goods or services and $40,000 for other goods and services. Additional procedures and reporting requirements apply to contracts under this exception.[9] Contracts that are subject to the bidding requirements (formal or informal) are not eligible for this exception and are therefore prohibited even if the other elements of this exception are present.[10]

A person who benefits from a contract under any of these exceptions is prohibited from participating in or voting on the contract.[11]

---

4. G.S. 14-234(a1)(4).

5. G.S. 14-234(b)(1).

6. G.S. 14-234(b)(2).

7. G.S. 14-234(b)(3).

8. G.S. 14-234(b)(4).

9. G.S. 14-234(d1).

10. G.S. 14-234(d2).

11. *See* G.S. 14-234(b1), -234(d1)(2).

4. Violation

It is a class 1 misdemeanor to violate G.S. 14-234, and any contract entered into in violation of this statute is void.[12]

5. Other Prohibitions

Other statutes contain prohibitions affecting particular types of local governments, including those which apply to public hospitals;[13] public hospital authorities;[14] city and county building inspectors;[15] redevelopment commission members and employees;[16] local management entity board members;[17] public housing authority members and employees;[18] and local alcoholic beverage control (ABC) board members.[19]

B. Prohibited Gifts and Favors (G.S. 133-32)

1. Prohibition

It is unlawful for certain contractors, subcontractors, or suppliers ("givers") to give gifts or offer favors to certain public officers or employees ("recipients"), or for these public officers or employees to accept such gifts or favors.[20]

2. Prohibited Givers

A prohibited giver is one who, with respect to any public agency,

(1) has a current contract;
(2) has performed under a contract within the past year; or
(3) anticipates bidding on a future contract.[21]

---

12. *See* G.S. 14-234(e), (f).
13. G.S. 131E-14.2.
14. G.S. 131E-21.
15. G.S. 160A-415; 153A-355.
16. G.S. 160A-511.
17. G.S. 122C-118.1(b).
18. G.S. 157-7.
19. G.S. 18B-201, -706.
20. G.S. 133-32(a).
21. *Id.*

3. Prohibited Recipients

A prohibited recipient is any officer or employee of the public agency who has responsibility for

(1) preparing plans, specifications, or estimates;
(2) awarding or administering contracts; or
(3) inspecting or supervising construction.[22]

4. Violation

It is a Class 1 misdemeanor to violate G.S. 133-32.[23]

5. Exceptions

Exemptions from the gifts and favors prohibition include the receipt of

(1) honorariums for participating in meetings;
(2) advertising items or souvenirs of nominal value;
(3) meals furnished at banquets;
(4) customary gifts or favors between employees or officers and their friends and relatives; and
(5) donations to support activities at meetings of professional organizations.[24]

Also, the statute does not prohibit governmental officials from participating in professional organization meeting activities if the activities are available to all of those attending the particular meeting.[25]

C. Restraint of Trade; Bid-Rigging (G.S. Chapter 133, Article 3)

It is a Class H felony for a person to engage in bid-rigging or other forms of restraint of trade relating to either a contract or a subcontract with a public agency that involves construction or repair work or supplying equipment, materials, goods, or services.[26] North Carolina courts may suspend from

---

22. *Id.*
23. G.S. 133-32(b).
24. G.S. 133-32(d).
25. *Id.*
26. G.S. 133-24, -25.

bidding, impose fines on, and revoke the licenses of any person convicted of bid-rigging/restraint of trade in this state.[27] Local governments may temporarily suspend from bidding any person who is charged with restraint of trade, and they may suspend those convicted of this offense in other states or in federal courts for up to three years.[28]

Local governments may require noncollusion affidavits from those who bid on their contracts,[29] and they may make information about their cost estimates and prospective bidders confidential prior to the receipt of bids.[30]

D. Misuse of Confidential Information (G.S. 14-234.1)

State law makes it unlawful for any state or local government officer or employee "in contemplation of official action by himself or by [the] governmental unit . . . , or in reliance on [confidential information received] in his official capacity," to acquire a pecuniary benefit or to aid another person to do so.[31] Violation of the confidential information statute is a Class 1 misdemeanor.[32]

E. Private Use of State's Purchasing System (G.S. 143-58.1)

Use of the state's purchasing system to secure goods or services for private and personal use is a Class 1 misdemeanor.[33] Exceptions apply for certain established policies and procedures that benefit a group or groups of people.[34]

---

27. G.S. 133-25.
28. G.S. 133-27.
29. G.S. 133-30.
30. G.S. 133-33.
31. G.S. 14-234.1(a).
32. G.S. 14-234.1(b).
33. G.S. 143-58.1(c).
34. G.S. 143-58.1(b).

F. Project Designer Financial Interest
(G.S. Chapter 133, Article 1)

Architects and engineers performing work on public construction projects are prohibited from specifying any materials, equipment, or other items manufactured, sold, or distributed by a company in which the project designer has a financial interest.[35] Project designers also are prohibited from allowing manufacturers to draw specifications for public construction projects.[36] A violation of these restrictions is punishable as a Class 3 misdemeanor; violators lose their licenses for one year and a pay a fine of up to $500.[37]

---

35. G.S. 133-1.
36. G.S. 133-2.
37. G.S. 133-4.

CHAPTER 6

Property Disposal

A. Basic Procedures (G.S. Chapter 160A, Article 12)

Chapter 160A, Article 12, of the North Carolina General Statutes (hereinafter G.S.) sets forth requirements and procedures for disposal of property by municipalities. Separate statutes make these procedures applicable to other local governments, including counties;[1] local school units;[2] community colleges;[3] sanitary districts;[4] local alcoholic beverage control (ABC) boards;[5] regional solid waste management authorities;[6] and municipal-owned airports.[7]

Procedures contained in these requirements apply based upon the type of property (real or personal) and the value of the property at the time of sale. Most methods of disposal require governing board approval and published notice. Except under a few limited circumstances, real property must always be sold using a competitive procedure.

---

1. Section 153A-176 of the North Carolina General Statutes (hereinafter G.S.).
2. G.S. 115C-518(a).
3. G.S. 115D-15.
4. G.S. 130A-55(20).
5. G.S. 18B-701(12).
6. G.S. 153A-427(b).
7. G.S. 63-53(4).

B. Competitive Sale (G.S. 160A-268 through -270)

Competitive procedures are required for most property disposal transactions and may be used in all instances, even if a special conveyance method is authorized. Three methods of competitive sale are authorized:

(1) sealed bid;[8]
(2) negotiated offer and upset bid;[9] and
(3) public auction (which includes electronic auction).[10]

C. Private Negotiation and Sale (G.S. 160A-266)

1. Small Surplus Items

Personal property valued at less than $30,000 may be sold by private negotiation and sale.[11] The governing board may delegate to an individual official or employee the authority to dispose of personal property valued at less than $30,000 and to use informal procedures designed to obtain fair market value for this property.[12]

2. Special Conveyances

Article 12 of G.S. Chapter 160A gives local governments the authority to dispose of both real and personal property by private negotiation and sale in specified instances, including when the disposal involves the following:

(1) Real and personal property with significant historical, cultural, artistic, or architectural characteristics[13]
(2) Real property sold in community development areas (cities only)[14]
(3) Real and personal property conveyed or leased when acquired for economic development purposes (cities and counties only)[15]

---

8. G.S. 160A-268.
9. G.S. 160A-269.
10. G.S. 160A-270.
11. G.S. 160A-266(b), -267.
12. G.S. 160A-266(c).
13. G.S. 160A-266(b).
14. G.S. 160A-457(4).
15. G.S. 159-7.1(d).

(4) Real and personal property conveyed for continued public use to nonprofit organizations to which the local government has the authority to appropriate funds (cities and counties only)[16]
(5) Personal property donated to other units of government, nonprofits, or sister cities[17]
(6) Real property conveyed to volunteer fire departments and rescue squads for facilities[18]

D. Conveyances between Governments (G.S. 160A-274)

State law authorizes governmental units to provide for the joint use of property, to sell or lease property to each other, or to exchange it with each other on a negotiated basis under terms and conditions "deem[ed] wise" by the governing board.[19]

E. Exchanges with Private Entities (G.S. 160A-271)

A local government may exchange real or personal property with real or personal property owned by a private individual or entity for full and fair consideration.

F. Leases (G.S. 160A-272)

Under G.S. 160A-272, a local government may lease or rent its real or personal property to a private entity or individual. Leases with a term of under one year may be entered into by the manager or by another employee authorized by the governing board. Leases for a term of between one and ten years require governing board approval. Any lease for a term greater than ten years must be treated as a sale of the property, with the exception of leases of up to twenty-five years for the siting and operation of renewable energy

---

16. G.S. 160A-279.
17. G.S. 160A-280.
18. G.S. 160A-277.
19. G.S. 160A-274(b).

facilities located on government property. The leasing of space at public airports is governed by G.S. 63-53.

G. Worthless Property (G.S. 160A-266(d))

A local government may discard property determined to have no value (1) which remains unsold or unclaimed after the unit has exhausted efforts to sell the property using any applicable procedure under G.S. Chapter 160A, Article 12 or (2) which poses a potential threat to public health or safety. No statutory procedures are required when discarding worthless property.

H. Trade-In (G.S. 143-129.7)

Under G.S. 143-129.7, a local government may dispose of personal property by including in the specifications for the purchase of apparatus, supplies, materials, or equipment an opportunity for a bidder to purchase as a "trade-in" other specified personal property, and the unit may award a contract for both the purchase and sale to the lowest responsive, responsible bidder, taking into consideration the trade-in amount offered in the bid. Property may be sold under this provision without separately complying with the otherwise applicable procedures of G.S. Chapter 160A, Article 12.

I. Public School Property (G.S. 115C-518(a))

Local boards of education follow G.S. Chapter 160A, Article 12 when disposing of real or personal property. When real property is disposed of, county governments must be offered a right of first refusal to purchase the property at fair market value. Real property also may be leased to another unit of government for $1 per year.[20] Local boards of education are constitutionally prohibited from donating real or personal property.[21]

---

20. G.S. 160A-274(c).
21. N.C. Const. art. IX, § 7; Boney v. Bd. of Trs., 229 N.C. 136, 48 S.E.2d 56 (1948).

J. Community College Property (G.S. 115D-15)

Community colleges follow Article 12 of G.S. Chapter 160A when disposing of real or personal property. Personal property may also be disposed of under procedures adopted by the North Carolina Department of Administration.[22] Property disposal procedures do not apply when a community college board of trustees conveys property to a county board of commissioners in connection with financing additions, improvements, renovations, and repairs to facilities.[23]

K. Seized, Forfeited, and Unclaimed Property (G.S. Chapter 15, Article 2)

Under Article 2 of G.S. Chapter 15, property seized or forfeited as a result of a criminal action; unclaimed property received by law enforcement (property that has been lost or stolen and not reclaimed by the owner); and abandoned bicycles must be sold at public auction after notice and a period during which the owners of such property may claim it. Abandoned bicycles may also be donated to a nonprofit organization if unclaimed by the owner after public notice.[24] The proceeds of these sales must be deposited in the county or city school fund.[25] Special procedures apply to the disposal of confiscated weapons and vary depending on the method of seizure and, in some instances, the criminal offense for which a defendant is convicted.[26]

L. Law Enforcement Officer Weapon and Badge (G.S. 20-187.2)

A governing board may convey a law enforcement officer's badge and service side arm to a retiring law enforcement officer or to the family of a law enforcement officer who was killed in the line of duty or who died while still

---

22. G.S. 115D-15(a).
23. G.S. 115D-15.1.
24. G.S. 15-12(b).
25. G.S. 15-15.
26. *See* G.S. 15-11.1(b1), -11.2; 14-269.1.

in active service. The officer's badge may be given for no consideration, and the board may set any price it chooses for the service side arm.

CHAPTER 7

Related Statutory Provisions

A. Accounting and Budgeting

The Local Government Budget and Fiscal Control Act[1] imposes a number of requirements that must be observed in the contracting process. For example, all contracts (including purchase orders) that obligate budgeted funds must be preaudited under Section 159-28(a) of the North Carolina General Statutes (hereinafter G.S.), and the local government's finance officer must certify in writing that the obligation is supported by an appropriation and that sufficient funds remain unencumbered to meet the obligation evidenced by the contract. The written preaudit certification must be affixed to the contract.

B. Installment-Purchase Contracts (G.S. 115C-528; 115D-58.15; 160A-20)

Cities, counties, and other specified local governments have broad authority to finance contracts over time and to create a security interest in the property purchased, subject to limitations established by statute.[2] Local school boards have authority to finance purchases (by installment- or by lease-purchase) only for automobiles, school buses, mobile classroom units, food service equipment, photocopiers, computers, computer hardware,

---

1. Sections 159-7 through -42 of the North Carolina General Statutes (hereinafter G.S.).
2. G.S. 160A-20.

computer software, and related support services.[3] Community colleges have installment- and lease-purchase authority for the purchase of equipment and real property.[4] Additional approval and procedural requirements and limitations (not discussed here) apply to these installment- or lease-purchase contracts for local school units and community colleges.

C. Continuing Contracts (G.S. 115C-432; 153A-13; 160A-17)

Municipalities,[5] counties,[6] and, implicitly, local school units[7] are authorized by statute to enter into continuing contracts—that is, contracts that extend beyond the current budget year.

D. Sales and Use Tax Refunds (G.S. 105-164.14(c))

Municipalities, counties, and a number of other local government entities (but not local school systems) are entitled to an annual refund of sales and use tax paid on the purchase of personal property and construction materials, supplies, equipment, and fixtures.

E. Writing Requirements (G.S. 22-2; 25-2-201; 143-129; 160A-16)

In all of the following circumstances, a contract must be in writing:

(1) When the contract is with a city[8]
(2) When the contract involves conveying real property, mining rights, or a lease with a term of three years or longer[9]

---

3. G.S. 115C-528.
4. G.S. 115D-15.
5. G.S. 160A-17.
6. G.S. 153A-13.
7. G.S. 115C-432(b)(4).
8. G.S. 160A-16.
9. G.S. 22-2.

(3) When the contract is for construction or repair work with an estimated cost of $500,000 or more[10]

(4) When the contract is a purchase contract with an estimated cost of $90,000 or more[11]

(5) When the contract is for the purchase of goods costing $500 or more[12]

(6) When the contract entails obligating public funds[13]

F. Contract Award (G.S. 143-129)

Whether or not the awarding of a contract requires governing board approval depends on the type of contract involved and the amount of that contract.

1. Construction or Repair Contracts in the Formal Bidding Range ($500,000 or More)

These types of contracts require governing board approval.[14]

2. Purchase Contracts in the Formal Bidding Range ($90,000 or More)

Contracts of this variety require governing board approval unless the governing board has delegated its approval authority to an individual officer or employee of the unit.[15]

3. Purchase and Construction or Repair Contracts in the Informal Bidding Range

No statutory requirements apply to the awarding of these kinds of contracts.

---

10. G.S. 143-129(c).

11. *Id.*

12. G.S. 25-2-201(1).

13. G.S. 159-28. *See also* Exec. Med. Transp., Inc. v Jones Cnty. Dep't of Soc. Servs., ___ N.C. App. ___, 735 S.E.2d 352 (2012), *discretionary review denied*, 366 N.C. 435 (2013).

14. G.S. 143-129(a).

15. *Id.*

G. Electronic Signatures (G.S. 66-58.12)

Electronic signatures are authorized and must satisfy specific statutory requirements.[16]

H. E-Verify (G.S. 143-129; 153A-449; 160A-20.1)

Local governments are prohibited from contracting with a contractor or vendor who has failed to comply with North Carolina's requirement that private employers who employ twenty-five or more workers in this state use the federal E-Verify system to confirm the legal eligibility to work of newly hired workers. For all units of local government, including cities and counties, the prohibition applies only to purchase and construction or repair contracts in the formal bidding range.[17]

I. Prohibited Contract Provisions (G.S. 22A-1; 22B-1 through -3 and -10; 143-133.5, -134.3; 153A-449; 160A-20.1)

Some contract provisions are barred by law. Terms and conditions that are considered to be against public policy and thus void by operation of statute include those that

(1) insulate a party from its own negligence under a construction indemnity agreement;[18]

(2) set the venue for disputes involving purchase of or improvements to real property exclusively in another state or require that the contract be governed by the laws of another state;[19]

(3) require the forum for litigation or arbitration be set in another state;[20]

(4) require a party to waive its right to a jury trial;[21]

---

16. *See* G.S. 66-58.1, -58.12.
17. G.S. 143-129(j); 160A-20.1(b); 153A-449(b).
18. G.S. 22B-1.
19. G.S. 22B-2.
20. G.S. 22B-3.
21. G.S. 22B-10.

(5) prohibit or limit compensable damages for delays on a construction project caused solely by the public owner;[22]

(6) require, prohibit, or discriminate against a bidder on a public construction contract for adhering or not adhering to a labor union agreement;[23] and

(7) impose as a condition of bidding an employment-related condition (such as minimum wage or paid sick leave) for which the local government lacks legal authority to impose on all private employers in its jurisdiction.[24]

---

22. G.S. 143-134.3.
23. G.S. 143-134.5.
24. G.S. 160A-20.1(a); 153A-449(a).

PART II

Selected General Statutes

Selected General Statutes

A. General Bidding Requirements

§ 143-129. Procedure for letting of public contracts.

(a) Bidding Required. - No construction or repair work requiring the estimated expenditure of public money in an amount equal to or more than five hundred thousand dollars ($500,000) or purchase of apparatus, supplies, materials, or equipment requiring an estimated expenditure of public money in an amount equal to or more than ninety thousand dollars ($90,000) may be performed, nor may any contract be awarded therefor, by any board or governing body of the State, or of any institution of the State government, or of any political subdivision of the State, unless the provisions of this section are complied with; provided that The University of North Carolina and its constituent institutions may award contracts for construction or repair work that requires an estimated expenditure of less than five hundred thousand dollars ($500,000) without complying with the provisions of this section.

For purchases of apparatus, supplies, materials, or equipment, the governing body of any political subdivision of the State may, subject to any restriction as to dollar amount, or other conditions that the governing body elects to impose, delegate to the manager, school superintendent, chief purchasing official, or other employee the authority to award contracts, reject bids, or readvertise to receive bids on behalf of the unit. Any person to whom authority is delegated under this subsection shall comply with the requirements of this Article that would otherwise apply to the governing body.

(b) Advertisement and Letting of Contracts. - Where the contract is to be let by a board or governing body of the State government or of a State institution, proposals shall be invited by advertisement in a newspaper having general circulation in the State of North Carolina. Where the contract is to be let by a political subdivision of the State, proposals shall be invited by advertisement in a newspaper having general circulation in the political subdivision or by electronic means, or both. A decision to advertise solely by electronic means, whether for particular contracts or generally for all contracts that are subject to this Article, shall be approved by the governing board of the political subdivision of the State at a regular meeting of the board.

The advertisements for bidders required by this section shall appear at a time where at least seven full days shall lapse between the date on which the notice appears and the date of the opening of bids. The advertisement shall: (i) state the time and place where plans and specifications of proposed work or a complete description of the apparatus, supplies, materials, or equipment may be had; (ii) state the time and place for opening of the proposals; and (iii) reserve to the board or governing body the right to reject any or all proposals.

Proposals may be rejected for any reason determined by the board or governing body to be in the best interest of the unit. However, the proposal shall not be rejected for the purpose of evading the provisions of this Article. No board or governing body of the State or political subdivision thereof may assume responsibility for construction or purchase contracts, or guarantee the payments of labor or materials therefor except under provisions of this Article.

All proposals shall be opened in public and the board or governing body shall award the contract to the lowest responsible bidder or bidders, taking into consideration quality, performance and the time specified in the proposals for the performance of the contract.

In the event the lowest responsible bids are in excess of the funds available for the project or purchase, the responsible board or governing body is authorized to enter into negotiations with the lowest responsible bidder above mentioned, making reasonable changes in the plans and specifications as may be necessary to bring the contract price within the funds available, and may award a contract to such bidder upon recommendation of the Department of Administration in the case of the State government or of a State institution or agency, or upon recommendation of the responsible commission, council or board in the case of a subdivision of the State, if such bidder will agree to perform the work or provide the apparatus, supplies, materials, or equipment at the negotiated price within the funds available therefor. If a contract cannot be let under the above conditions, the board or governing body is authorized to readvertise, as herein provided, after having made such changes in plans and specifications as may be necessary to bring the cost of the project or purchase within the funds available therefor. The procedure above specified may be repeated if necessary in order to secure an acceptable contract within the funds available therefor.

No proposal for construction or repair work may be considered or accepted by said board or governing body unless at the time of its filing the same shall be accompanied by a deposit with said board or governing body of cash, or a cashier's check, or a certified check on some bank or trust company insured by the Federal Deposit Insurance Corporation in an amount equal to not less than five percent (5%) of the proposal. In lieu of making the cash deposit as above provided, such bidder may file a bid bond executed by a corporate surety licensed under the laws of North Carolina to execute such bonds, conditioned that the surety will upon demand forthwith make payment to the obligee upon said bond if the bidder fails to execute the contract in accordance with the bid bond. This deposit shall be retained if the successful bidder fails to execute the contract within 10 days after the award or fails to give satisfactory surety as required herein.

Bids shall be sealed and the opening of an envelope or package with knowledge that it contains a bid or the disclosure or exhibition of the contents of any bid by anyone without the permission of the bidder prior to the time set for opening in the invitation to bid shall constitute a Class 1 misdemeanor.

(c)   Contract Execution and Security. - All contracts to which this section applies shall be executed in writing. The board or governing body shall require the person to whom the award of a contract for construction or repair work is made to furnish bond as required by Article 3 of Chapter 44A; or require a deposit of money, certified check or government securities for the full amount of said contract to secure the faithful performance of the terms of said contract and the payment of all sums due for labor and materials in a manner consistent with Article 3 of Chapter 44A; and the contract shall not be altered except by written agreement of the contractor and the board or governing body. The surety bond or deposit required herein shall be deposited with the board or governing body for which the work is to be performed. When a deposit, other than a surety bond, is made with the board or governing body, the board or governing body assumes all the liabilities, obligations and duties of a surety as provided in Article 3 of Chapter 44A to the extent of said deposit.

The owning agency or the Department of Administration, in contracts involving a State agency, and the owning agency or the governing board, in contracts involving a political subdivision of the State, may reject the bonds of any surety company against which there is pending any unsettled claim or complaint made by a State agency or the owning agency or governing board of any political subdivision of the State arising out of any contract under which State funds, in contracts with the State, or funds of political subdivisions of the State, in contracts with such political subdivision, were expended, provided such claim or complaint has been pending more than 180 days.

(d) Use of Unemployment Relief Labor. - Nothing in this section shall operate so as to require any public agency to enter into a contract which will prevent the use of unemployment relief labor paid for in whole or in part by appropriations or funds furnished by the State or federal government.

(e) Exceptions. - The requirements of this Article do not apply to:

(1) The purchase, lease, or other acquisition of any apparatus, supplies, materials, or equipment from: (i) the United States of America or any agency thereof; or (ii) any other government unit or agency thereof within the United States. The Secretary of Administration or the governing board of any political subdivision of the State may designate any officer or employee of the State or political subdivision to enter a bid or bids in its behalf at any sale of apparatus, supplies, materials, equipment, or other property owned by: (i) the United States of America or any agency thereof; or (ii) any other governmental unit or agency thereof within the United States. The Secretary of Administration or the governing board of any political subdivision of the State may authorize the officer or employee to make any partial or down payment or payment in full that may be required by regulations of the governmental unit or agency disposing of the property.

(2) Cases of special emergency involving the health and safety of the people or their property.

(3) Purchases made through a competitive bidding group purchasing program, which is a formally organized program that offers competitively obtained purchasing services at discount prices to two or more public agencies.

(4) Construction or repair work undertaken during the progress of a construction or repair project initially begun pursuant to this section.

(5) Purchase of gasoline, diesel fuel, alcohol fuel, motor oil, fuel oil, or natural gas. These purchases are subject to G.S. 143-131.

(6) Purchases of apparatus, supplies, materials, or equipment when: (i) performance or price competition for a product are not available; (ii) a needed product is available from only one source of supply; or (iii) standardization or compatibility is the overriding consideration. Notwithstanding any other provision of this section, the governing board of a political subdivision of the State shall approve the purchases listed in the preceding sentence prior to the award of the contract.

In the case of purchases by hospitals, in addition to the other exceptions in this subsection, the provisions of this Article shall not apply when: (i) a particular medical item or prosthetic appliance is needed; (ii) a particular product is ordered by an attending physician for his patients; (iii) additional products are needed to complete an ongoing job or task; (iv) products are purchased for "over-the-counter" resale; (v) a particular product is needed or desired for experimental, developmental, or research work; or (vi) equipment is already installed, connected, and in service under a lease or other agreement and the governing body of the hospital determines that the equipment should be purchased. The governing body of a hospital shall keep a record of all purchases made pursuant to this subdivision. These records are subject to public inspection.

(7) Purchases of information technology through contracts established by the State Office of Information Technology Services as provided in G.S. 147-33.82(b) and G.S. 147-33.92(b).

(8) Guaranteed energy savings contracts, which are governed by Article 3B of Chapter 143 of the General Statutes.

(9) Purchases from contracts established by the State or any agency of the State, if the contractor is willing to extend to a political subdivision of the State the same or more favorable prices, terms, and conditions as established in the State contract.

(9a) Purchases of apparatus, supplies, materials, or equipment from contracts established by the United States of America or any federal agency, if the contractor is willing to extend to a political subdivision of the State the same or more favorable prices, terms, and conditions as established in the federal contract.

(10) Purchase of used apparatus, supplies, materials, or equipment. For purposes of this subdivision, remanufactured, refabricated or demo apparatus, supplies, materials, or equipment are not included in the exception. A demo item is one that is used for demonstration and is sold by the manufacturer or retailer at a discount.

(11) Contracts by a public entity with a construction manager at risk executed pursuant to G.S. 143-128.1.

(12) (Repealed effective July 1, 2015) Build-to-suit capital leases with a private developer under G.S. 115C-532.

(f) Repealed by Session Laws 2001-328, s. 1, effective August 2, 2001.

(g) Waiver of Bidding for Previously Bid Contracts. - When the governing board of any political subdivision of the State, or the person to whom authority has been delegated under subsection (a) of this section, determines that it is in the best interest of the unit, the requirements of this section may be waived for the purchase of apparatus, supplies, materials, or equipment from any person or entity that has, within the previous 12 months, after having completed a public, formal bid process substantially similar to that required by this Article, contracted to furnish the apparatus, supplies, materials, or equipment to:

(1) The United States of America or any federal agency;

(2) The State of North Carolina or any agency or political subdivision of the State; or

(3) Any other state or any agency or political subdivision of that state, if the person or entity is willing to furnish the items at the same or more favorable prices, terms, and conditions as those provided under the contract with the other unit or agency. Notwithstanding any other provision of this section, any purchase made under this subsection shall be approved by the governing body of the purchasing political subdivision of the State at a regularly scheduled meeting of the governing

body no fewer than 10 days after publication of notice that a waiver of the bid procedure will be considered in order to contract with a qualified supplier pursuant to this section. Notice may be published in a newspaper having general circulation in the political subdivision or by electronic means, or both. A decision to publish notice solely by electronic means for a particular contract or for all contracts under this subsection shall be approved by the governing board of the political subdivision. Rules issued by the Secretary of Administration pursuant to G.S. 143-49(6) shall apply with respect to participation in State term contracts.

(h)   Transportation Authority Purchases. - Notwithstanding any other provision of this section, any board or governing body of any regional public transportation authority, hereafter referred to as a "RPTA," created pursuant to Article 26 of Chapter 160A of the General Statutes, or a regional transportation authority, hereafter referred to as a "RTA," created pursuant to Article 27 of Chapter 160A of the General Statutes, may approve the entering into of any contract for the purchase, lease, or other acquisition of any apparatus, supplies, materials, or equipment without competitive bidding and without meeting the requirements of subsection (b) of this section if the following procurement by competitive proposal (Request for Proposal) method is followed.

The competitive proposal method of procurement is normally conducted with more than one source submitting an offer or proposal. Either a fixed price or cost reimbursement type contract is awarded. This method of procurement is generally used when conditions are not appropriate for the use of sealed bids. If this procurement method is used, all of the following requirements apply:

(1)   Requests for proposals shall be publicized. All evaluation factors shall be identified along with their relative importance.

(2)   Proposals shall be solicited from an adequate number of qualified sources.

(3)   RPTAs or RTAs shall have a method in place for conducting technical evaluations of proposals received and selecting awardees, with the goal of promoting fairness and competition without requiring strict adherence to specifications or price in determining the most advantageous proposal.

(4) The award may be based upon initial proposals without further discussion or negotiation or, in the discretion of the evaluators, discussions or negotiations may be conducted either with all offerors or with those offerors determined to be within the competitive range, and one or more revised proposals or a best and final offer may be requested of all remaining offerors. The details and deficiencies of an offeror's proposal may not be disclosed to other offerors during any period of negotiation or discussion.

(5) The award shall be made to the responsible firm whose proposal is most advantageous to the RPTA's or the RTA's program with price and other factors considered.

The contents of the proposals shall not be public records until 14 days before the award of the contract.

The board or governing body of the RPTA or the RTA shall, at the regularly scheduled meeting, by formal motion make findings of fact that the procurement by competitive proposal (Request for Proposals) method of procuring the particular apparatus, supplies, materials, or equipment is the most appropriate acquisition method prior to the issuance of the requests for proposals and shall by formal motion certify that the requirements of this subsection have been followed before approving the contract.

Nothing in this subsection subjects a procurement by competitive proposal under this subsection to G.S. 143-49, 143-52, or 143-53.

RPTAs and RTAs may adopt regulations to implement this subsection.

(i) Procedure for Letting of Public Contracts. - The Department of Transportation ("DOT"), The University of North Carolina and its constituent institutions ("UNC"), and the Department of Administration ("DOA") shall monitor all projects in those agencies and institutions that are let without a performance or payment bond to determine the number of defaults on those projects, the cost to complete each defaulted project, and each project's contract price. Beginning March 1, 2011, and annually thereafter, DOT, UNC, and DOA shall report this information to the Joint Legislative Committee on Governmental Operations.

(j) [Use of E-Verify Required. -] No contract subject to this section may be awarded by any board or governing body of the State, institution of State government, or any political subdivision of the State unless the contractor and the contractor's subcontractors comply with the requirements of Article 2 of Chapter 64 of the General Statutes.

§ 143-129.1. Withdrawal of bid.

A public agency may allow a bidder submitting a bid pursuant to G.S. 143-129 for construction or repair work or for the purchase of apparatus, supplies, materials, or equipment to withdraw his bid from consideration after the bid opening without forfeiture of his bid security if the price bid was based upon a mistake, which constituted a substantial error, provided the bid was submitted in good faith, and the bidder submits credible evidence that the mistake was clerical in nature as opposed to a judgment error, and was actually due to an unintentional and substantial arithmetic error or an unintentional omission of a substantial quantity of work, labor, apparatus, supplies, materials, equipment, or services made directly in the compilation of the bid, which unintentional arithmetic error or unintentional omission can be clearly shown by objective evidence drawn from inspection of the original work papers, documents or materials used in the preparation of the bid sought to be withdrawn. A request to withdraw a bid must be made in writing to the public agency which invited the proposals for the work prior to the award of the contract, but not later than 72 hours after the opening of bids, or for a longer period as may be specified in the instructions to bidders provided prior to the opening of bids.

If a request to withdraw a bid has been made in accordance with the provisions of this section, action on the remaining bids shall be considered, in accordance with North Carolina G.S. 143-129, as though said bid had not been received. Notwithstanding the foregoing, such bid shall be deemed to have been received for the purpose of complying with the requirements of G.S. 143-132. If the work or purchase is relet for bids, under no circumstances may the bidder who has filed a request to withdraw be permitted to rebid the work or purchase.

If a bidder files a request to withdraw his bid, the agency shall promptly hold a hearing thereon. The agency shall give to the withdrawing bidder reasonable notice of the time and place of any such hearing. The bidder, either in person or through counsel, may appear at the hearing and present any additional facts and arguments in support of his request to withdraw his bid. The agency shall issue a written ruling allowing or denying the request to withdraw within five days after the hearing. If the agency finds that the price bid was based upon a mistake of the type described in the first paragraph of this section, then the agency shall issue a ruling permitting the bidder to withdraw without forfeiture of the bidder's security. If the agency finds that the price bid was based upon a mistake not of the type described in the first paragraph of this section, then the agency shall issue a ruling denying the request to withdraw and requiring the forfeiture of the bidder's security. A denial by the agency of the request to withdraw a bid shall have the same effect as if an award had been made to the bidder and a refusal by the bidder to accept had been made, or as if there had been a refusal to enter into the contract, and the bidder's bid deposit or bid bond shall be forfeited.

In the event said ruling denies the request to withdraw the bid, the bidder shall have the right, within 20 days after receipt of said ruling, to contest the matter by the filing of a civil action in any court of competent jurisdiction of the State of North Carolina. The procedure shall be the same as in all civil actions except all issues of law and fact and every other issue shall be tried de novo by the judge without jury; provided that the matter may be referred in the instances and in the manner provided for by North Carolina G.S. 1A-1, Rule 53, as amended. Notwithstanding the foregoing, if the public agency involved is the Department of Administration, it may follow its normal rules and regulations with respect to contested matters, as opposed to following the administrative procedures set forth herein. If it is finally determined that the bidder did not have the right to withdraw his bid pursuant to the provisions of this section, the bidder's security shall be forfeited. Every bid bond or bid deposit given by a bidder to a public agency pursuant to G.S. 143-129 shall be conclusively presumed to have been given in accordance with this section, whether or not it be so drawn as to conform to this section. This section shall be conclusively presumed to have been written into every bid bond given pursuant to G.S. 143-129.

Neither the agency nor any elected or appointed official, employee, representative or agent of such agency shall incur any liability or surcharge, in the absence of fraud or collusion, by permitting the withdrawal of a bid pursuant to the provisions of this section.

No withdrawal of the bid which would result in the award of the contract on another bid of the same bidder, his partner, or to a corporation or business venture owned by or in which he has an interest shall be permitted. No bidder who is permitted to withdraw a bid shall supply any material or labor to, or perform any subcontract or work agreement for, any person to whom a contract or subcontract is awarded in the performance of the contract for which the withdrawn bid was submitted, without the prior written approval of the agency. Whoever violates the provisions of the foregoing sentence shall be guilty of a Class 1 misdemeanor.

§ 143-129.8. Purchase of information technology goods and services.

(a)　In recognition of the complex and innovative nature of information technology goods and services and of the desirability of a single point of responsibility for contracts that include combinations of purchase of goods, design, installation, training, operation, maintenance, and related services, a political subdivision of the State may contract for information technology, as defined in G.S. 147-33.81(2), using the procedure set forth in this section, in addition to or instead of any other procedure available under North Carolina law.

(b)　Contracts for information technology may be entered into under a request for proposals procedure that satisfies the following minimum requirements:

(1)　Notice of the request for proposals shall be given in accordance with G.S. 143-129(b).

(2)　Contracts shall be awarded to the person or entity that submits the best overall proposal as determined by the awarding authority. Factors to be considered in awarding contracts shall be identified in the request for proposals.

(c)　The awarding authority may use procurement methods set forth in G.S. 143-135.9 in developing and evaluating requests for proposals under this section. The awarding authority may negotiate with any proposer in order to obtain a final contract that best meets the needs of the awarding authority. Negotiations allowed under this section shall not alter the contract beyond the scope of the original request for proposals in a manner that: (i) deprives the proposers or potential proposers of a fair opportunity to compete for the contract; and (ii) would have resulted in the award of the contract to a different person or entity if the alterations had been included in the request for proposals.

(d)　Proposals submitted under this section shall not be subject to public inspection until a contract is awarded.

§ 143-129.9. Alternative competitive bidding methods.

(a)   A political subdivision of the State may use any of the following methods to obtain competitive bids for the purchase of apparatus, supplies, materials, or equipment as an alternative to the otherwise applicable requirements in this Article:

    (1)   Reverse auction. - For purposes of this section, "reverse auction" means a real-time purchasing process in which bidders compete to provide goods at the lowest selling price in an open and interactive environment. The bidders' prices may be revealed during the reverse auction. A reverse auction may be conducted by the political subdivision or by a third party under contract with the political subdivision. A political subdivision may also conduct a reverse auction through the State electronic procurement system, and compliance with the procedures and requirements of the State's reverse auction process satisfies the political subdivision's obligations under this Article.

    (2)   Electronic bidding. - A political subdivision may receive bids electronically in addition to or instead of paper bids. Procedures for receipt of electronic bids for contracts that are subject to the requirements of G.S. 143-129 shall be designed to ensure the security, authenticity, and confidentiality of the bids to at least the same extent as is provided for with sealed paper bids.

(b)   The requirements for advertisement of bidding opportunities, timeliness of the receipt of bids, the standard for the award of contracts, and all other requirements in this Article that are not inconsistent with the methods authorized in this section shall apply to contracts awarded under this section.

(c)   Reverse auctions shall not be utilized for the purchase or acquisition of construction aggregates, including, but not limited to, crushed stone, sand, and gravel.

§ 143-131. When counties, cities, towns and other subdivisions may let contracts on informal bids.

(a)   All contracts for construction or repair work or for the purchase of apparatus, supplies, materials, or equipment, involving the expenditure of public money in the amount of thirty thousand dollars ($30,000) or more, but less than the limits prescribed in G.S. 143-129, made by any officer, department, board, local school administrative unit, or commission of any county, city, town, or other subdivision of this State shall be made after informal bids have been secured. All such contracts shall be awarded to the lowest responsible, responsive bidder, taking into consideration quality, performance, and the time specified in the bids for the performance of the contract. It shall be the duty of any officer, department, board, local school administrative unit, or commission entering into such contract to keep a record of all bids submitted, and such record shall not be subject to public inspection until the contract has been awarded.

(b)   All public entities shall solicit minority participation in contracts for the erection, construction, alteration or repair of any building awarded pursuant to this section. The public entity shall maintain a record of contractors solicited and shall document efforts to recruit minority business participation in those contracts. Nothing in this section shall be construed to require formal advertisement of bids. All data, including the type of project, total dollar value of the project, dollar value of minority business participation on each project, and documentation of efforts to recruit minority participation shall be reported to the Department of Administration, Office for Historically Underutilized Business, upon the completion of the project.

§ 143-133. No evasion permitted.

No bill or contract shall be divided for the purpose of evading the provisions of this Article.

§ 143-135.9. Best Value procurements.

(a)   Definitions. - The following definitions apply in this section:

(1)   Best Value procurement. - The selection of a contractor based on a determination of which proposal offers the best trade-off between price and performance, where quality is considered an integral performance factor. The award decision is made based on multiple factors, including: total cost of ownership, meaning the cost of acquiring, operating, maintaining, and supporting a product or service over its projected lifetime; the evaluated technical merit of the vendor's proposal; the vendor's past performance; and the evaluated probability of

performing the requirements stated in the solicitation on time, with high quality, and in a manner that accomplishes the stated business objectives and maintains industry standards compliance.

(2) Government-Vendor partnership. - A mutually beneficial contractual relationship between State government and a contractor, wherein the two share risk and reward, and value is added to the procurement of needed goods or services.

(3) Repealed by Session Laws 2013-188, s. 1, effective June 26, 2013.

(4) Solution-Based solicitation. - A solicitation in which the requirements are stated in terms of how the product or service being purchased should accomplish the business objectives, rather than in terms of the technical design of the product or service.

(b) Intent. - The intent of Best Value procurement is to enable contractors to offer and the agency to select the most appropriate solution to meet the business objectives defined in the solicitation and to keep all parties focused on the desired outcome of a procurement.

(c) Information Technology. - The acquisition of information technology by the State of North Carolina shall be conducted using the Best Value procurement method. For purposes of this section, business process reengineering, system design, and technology implementation may be combined into a single solicitation. For acquisitions which the procuring agency and the Division of Purchase and Contracts or the Office of Information Technology Services, as applicable, deem to be highly complex or determine that the optimal solution to the business problem at hand is not known, the use of Solution-Based Solicitation and Government-Vendor Partnership is authorized and encouraged. Any county, city, town, or subdivision of the State may acquire information technology pursuant to this section.

(d) Repealed by Session Laws 2009-320, s. 1, effective July 24, 2009.

(e) North Carolina Zoological Park. - The acquisition of goods and services under a contract entered pursuant to the exemption of G.S. 143-129.8A(a) by the Department of Environment and Natural Resources on behalf of the North Carolina Zoological Park may be conducted using the Best Value procurement method. For acquisitions which the procuring agency deems to be highly complex, the use of Government-Vendor partnership is authorized.

§ 160A-19. Leases.

A city is authorized to lease as lessee, with or without option to purchase, any real or personal property for any authorized public purpose. A lease of personal property with an option to purchase is subject to Article 8 of Chapter 143 of the General Statutes.

§ 153A-165. Leases.

A county may lease as lessee, with or without option to purchase, any real or personal property for any authorized public purpose. A lease of personal property with an option to purchase is subject to Chapter 143, Article 8.

§ 115C-264. Operation.

(a)   In the operation of their public school nutrition programs, the public schools shall participate in the National School Lunch Program established by the federal government. The program shall be under the jurisdiction of the Division of School Support, Child Nutrition Services of the Department of Public Instruction and in accordance with federal guidelines as established by the Food and Nutrition Service of the United States Department of Agriculture.

(b)   For nutritional purposes, the public schools shall not (i) use cooking oils in their school food programs that contain trans-fatty acids or (ii) sell processed foods containing trans-fatty acids that were formed during the commercial processing of the foods.

(c)   All school food services shall be operated on a nonprofit basis, and any earnings therefrom over and above the cost of operation as defined herein shall be used to reduce the cost of food, to serve better food, or to provide free or reducedprice lunches to indigent children and for no other purpose. The term "cost of operation" means the actual cost incurred in the purchase and preparation of food, the salaries of all personnel directly engaged in providing food services, and the cost of nonfood supplies as outlined under standards adopted by the State Board of Education. "Personnel" means child nutrition supervisors or directors, bookkeepers directly engaged in food service record keeping and those persons directly involved in preparing and serving food. Child nutrition personnel shall be paid from the funds of food services only for services rendered in behalf of the child nutrition program. Any cost incurred in the provisions and maintenance of school food services over and beyond the cost of operation shall be included in the budget request filed annually by local boards of education with boards of county commissioners. Public schools are not required to comply with G.S. 115C-522(a) in the purchase of supplies and food for such school food services.

§ 115C-522. Provision of equipment for buildings.

(a)   It shall be the duty of local boards of education to purchase or exchange all supplies, equipment, and materials, and these purchases shall be made in accordance with Article 8 of Chapter 143 of the General Statutes. These purchases may be made from contracts made by the Department of Administration. Title to instructional supplies, office supplies, fuel and janitorial supplies, enumerated in the current expense fund budget and purchased out of State funds, shall be taken in the name of the local board of education which shall be responsible for the custody and replacement: Provided, that no contracts shall be made by any local school administrative unit for purchases unless provision has been made in the budget of the unit to pay for the purchases, unless surplus funds are on hand to pay for the purchases, or unless the contracts are made pursuant to G.S. 115C-47(28) and G.S. 115C-528 and adequate funds are available to pay in the current fiscal year the sums obligated for the current fiscal year. The State Board of Education shall adopt rules regarding equipment standards for supplies, equipment, and materials related to student transportation. The State Board may adopt guidelines for any commodity that needs safety features. If a commodity that needs safety features is available on statewide term contract, any guidelines adopted by the State Board must at a minimum meet the safety standards of the statewide term contract. Compliance with Article 8 of Chapter 143 of the General Statutes is not mandatory for the purchase of published books, manuscripts, maps, pamphlets, and periodicals.

    (1)   Where competition is available, local school administrative units may utilize the:

        a.   E-Quote service of the NC E-Procurement system as one means of solicitation in seeking informal bids for purchases subject to the bidding requirements of G.S. 143-131; and

b. Division of Purchase and Contract's electronic Interactive Purchasing System as one means of advertising formal bids on purchases subject to the bidding requirements of G.S. 143-129 and applicable rules regarding advertising. This sub-subdivision does not prohibit a local school administrative unit from using other methods of advertising.

(2) In order to provide an efficient transition of purchasing procedures, the Secretary of the Department of Administration and the local school administrative units shall establish a local school administrative unit purchasing user group. The user group shall be comprised of a proportionate number of representatives from the Department of Administration and local school administrative unit purchasing and finance officers. The user group shall examine any issues that may arise between the Department of Administration and local school administrative units, including the new relationship between the Department and the local school administrative units, the appropriate exchange of information, the continued efficient use of E-Procurement, appropriate bid procedures, and any other technical assistance that may be necessary for the purchase of supplies and materials.

(b) It shall be the duty of the local boards of education to provide suitable school furniture and apparatus, as provided in G.S. 115C-521(b).

(c) It shall be the duty of local boards of education and taxlevying authorities to provide suitable supplies for the school buildings under their jurisdictions. These shall include, in addition to the necessary instructional supplies, proper window shades, blackboards, reference books, library equipment, maps, and equipment for teaching the sciences.

Likewise, it shall be the duty of said boards of education and boards of county commissioners to provide every school with a good supply of water, approved by the Department of Environment and Natural Resources, and where such school cannot be connected to watercarried sewerage facilities, there shall be provided sanitary privies for the boys and for the girls according to specifications of the Commission for Public Health. Such water supply and sanitary privies shall be considered an essential and necessary part of the equipment of each public school and may be paid for in the same manner as desks and other essential equipment of the school are paid for.

§ 115D-58.5. Accounting system.

(a) Each institution shall establish and maintain an accounting system consistent with procedures as prescribed by the Community Colleges System Office and the State Controller, which shows its assets, liabilities, equities, revenues, and expenditures.

(b) Each institution shall be governed in its purchasing of all supplies, equipment, and materials by contracts made by or with the approval of the Purchase and Contract Division of the Department of Administration except as provided in G.S. 115D-58.14. No contract shall be made by any board of trustees for purchases unless provision has been made in the budget of the institution to provide payment thereof. In order to protect the State purchase contracts, it is the duty of the board of trustees and administrative officers of each institution to pay for such purchases promptly in accordance with the contract of purchase. Equipment shall be titled to the State Board of Community Colleges if derived from State or federal funds.

(c) The operations of each institution shall be subject to oversight of the State Auditor pursuant to Article 5A of Chapter 147 of the General Statutes.

(d) Repealed by Session Laws 1983, c. 913, s. 18.

§ 115D-58.14. Purchasing flexibility.

(a) Community colleges may purchase supplies, equipment, and materials from noncertified sources that are available under State term contracts, subject to the following conditions:

(1) The purchase price, including the cost of delivery, is less than the cost under the State term contract;

(2) The cost of the purchase shall not exceed the bid value benchmark established under G.S. 143-53.1; and

(3) The items are the same or substantially similar in quality, service, and performance as items available under State term contracts.

(a1) Notwithstanding the provisions of this section, a community college may purchase, in any lawful manner, an item that is neither available under State term contracts nor substantially similar to an item available under State term contracts.

(b)   The State Board of Community Colleges and the Department of Administration shall jointly adopt policies and procedures for monitoring the implementation of this section, including without limitation (i) definitions of substantial similarity, (ii) the content and frequency of reports and audits of such purchases, and (iii) a process for identifying any term contract existing as of October 1, 2009, with respect to which the exercise of purchasing flexibility could constitute a breach of that contract.

In the formation of each new term contract entered into after October 1, 2009, the Department of Administration shall, in its discretion, either provide in the contract for the purchasing flexibility set out in this section or make the term contract inapplicable to community colleges.

(c)   The State Board of Community Colleges, in consultation with the Department of Administration, shall review the purchasing process for community colleges and may increase or decrease the purchasing/delegation benchmark for each community college based on the college's overall capabilities, including staff resources, purchasing compliance reviews, and audit reports. The State Board may, in its discretion, reduce a community college's purchasing/delegation benchmark at anytime. The State Board shall not increase a community college's purchasing/delegation benchmark by more than fifteen percent (15%) in any calendar year without the concurrence of the Department of Administration within 60 days of submission. The maximum purchasing/delegation benchmark for a community college shall be one hundred thousand dollars ($100,000).

B. Additional Requirements for Construction Contracts

§ 143-128. Requirements for certain building contracts.

(a)   Preparation of specifications. - Every officer, board, department, commission or commissions charged with responsibility of preparation of specifications or awarding or entering into contracts for the erection, construction, alteration or repair of any buildings for the State, or for any county, municipality, or other public body, shall have prepared separate specifications for each of the following subdivisions or branches of work to be performed:

(1) Heating, ventilating, air conditioning and accessories (separately or combined into one conductive system), refrigeration for cold storage (where the cold storage cooling load is 15 tons or more of refrigeration), and all related work.

(2) Plumbing and gas fittings and accessories, and all related work.

(3) Electrical wiring and installations, and all related work.

(4) General work not included in subdivisions (1), (2), and (3) of this subsection relating to the erection, construction, alteration, or repair of any building.

Specifications for contracts that will be bid under the separate-prime system or dual bidding system shall be drawn as to permit separate and independent bidding upon each of the subdivisions of work enumerated in this subsection. The above enumeration of subdivisions or branches of work shall not be construed to prevent any officer, board, department, commission or commissions from preparing additional separate specifications for any other category of work.

(a1) Construction methods. - The State, a county, municipality, or other public body shall award contracts to erect, construct, alter, or repair buildings pursuant to any of the following methods:

(1) Separate-prime bidding.

(2) Single-prime bidding.

(3) Dual bidding pursuant to subsection (d1) of this section.

(4) Construction management at risk contracts pursuant to G.S. 143-128.1.

(5) Alternative contracting methods authorized pursuant to G.S. 143-135.26(9).

(6) Design-build contracts pursuant to G.S. 143-128.1A.

(7) Design-build bridging contracts pursuant to G.S. 143-128.1B.

(8) Public-private partnership construction contracts pursuant to G.S. 143-128.1C.

(a2) Repealed by Session Laws 2012-142, s. 9.4(g), effective July 1, 2012.

(b) Separate-prime contracts. - When the State, county, municipality, or other public body uses the separate-prime contract system, it shall accept bids for each subdivision of work for which specifications are required to be prepared under subsection (a) of this section and shall award the respective work specified separately to responsible and reliable persons, firms or corporations regularly engaged in their respective lines of work. When the estimated cost of work to be performed in any single subdivision or branch for which separate bids are required by this subsection is less than twenty-five thousand dollars ($25,000), the same may be included in the contract for one of the other subdivisions or branches of the work, irrespective of total project cost. The contracts shall be awarded to the lowest responsible, responsive bidders, taking into consideration quality, performance, the time specified in the bids for performance of the contract, and compliance with G.S. 143-128.2. Bids may also be accepted from and awards made to separate contractors for other categories of work.

Each separate contractor shall be directly liable to the State of North Carolina, or to the county, municipality, or other public body and to the other separate contractors for the full performance of all duties and obligations due respectively under the terms of the separate contracts and in accordance with the plans and specifications, which shall specifically set forth the duties and obligations of each separate contractor. For the purpose of this section, "separate contractor" means any person, firm or corporation who shall enter into a contract with the State, or with any county, municipality, or other public entity to erect, construct, alter or repair any building or buildings, or parts of any building or buildings.

(c)　Repealed by Session Laws 2001-496, s. 3, effective January 1, 2001.

(d)　Single-prime contracts. - All bidders in a single-prime project shall identify on their bid the contractors they have selected for the subdivisions or branches of work for:

(1)　Heating, ventilating, and air conditioning;

(2)　Plumbing;

(3)　Electrical; and

(4)　General.

The contract shall be awarded to the lowest responsible, responsive bidder, taking into consideration quality, performance, the time specified in the bids for performance of the contract, and compliance with G.S. 143-128.2. A contractor whose bid is accepted shall not substitute any person as subcontractor in the place of the subcontractor listed in the original bid, except (i) if the listed subcontractor's bid is later determined by the contractor to be nonresponsible or nonresponsive or the listed subcontractor refuses to enter into a contract for the complete performance of the bid work, or (ii) with the approval of the awarding authority for good cause shown by the contractor. The terms, conditions, and requirements of each contract between the contractor and a subcontractor performing work under a subdivision or branch of work listed in this subsection shall incorporate by reference the terms, conditions, and requirements of the contract between the contractor and the State, county, municipality, or other public body.

When contracts are awarded pursuant to this section, the public body shall make available to subcontractors the dispute resolution process as provided for in subsection (f1) of this section.

(d1) Dual bidding. - The State, a county, municipality, or other public entity may accept bids to erect, construct, alter, or repair a building under both the single-prime and separate-prime contracting systems and shall award the contract to the lowest responsible, responsive bidder under the single-prime system or to the lowest responsible, responsive bidder under the separate-prime system, taking into consideration quality, performance, compliance with G.S. 143-128.2, and time specified in the bids to perform the contract. In determining the system under which the contract will be awarded to the lowest responsible, responsive bidder, the public entity may consider cost of construction oversight, time for completion, and other factors it considers appropriate. The bids received as separate-prime bids shall be received, but not opened, one hour prior to the deadline for the submission of single-prime bids. The amount of a bid submitted by a subcontractor to the general contractor under the single-prime system shall not exceed the amount bid, if any, for the same work by that subcontractor to the public entity under the separate-prime system. The provisions of subsection (b) of this section shall apply to separate-prime contracts awarded pursuant to this section and the provisions of subsection (d) of this section shall apply to single-prime contracts awarded pursuant to this section.

(e) Project expediter; scheduling; public body to resolve project disputes. - The State, county, municipality, or other public body may, if specified in the bid documents, provide for assignment of responsibility for expediting the work on a project to a single responsible and reliable person, firm or corporation, which may be a prime contractor. In executing this responsibility, the designated project expediter may recommend to the State, county, municipality, or other public body whether payment to a contractor should be approved. The project expediter, if required by the contract documents, shall be responsible for preparing the project schedule and shall allow all contractors and subcontractors performing any of the branches of work listed in subsection (d) of this section equal input into the preparation of the initial schedule. Whenever separate contracts are awarded and separate contractors engaged for a project pursuant to this section, the public body may provide in the contract documents for resolution of project disputes through alternative dispute resolution processes as provided for in subsection (f1) of this section.

(f)   Repealed by Session Laws 2001-496, s. 3, effective January 1, 2001.

(f1)   Dispute resolution. - A public entity shall use the dispute resolution process adopted by the State Building Commission pursuant to G.S. 143-135.26(11), or shall adopt another dispute resolution process, which shall include mediation, to be used as an alterative to the dispute resolution process adopted by the State Building Commission. This dispute resolution process will be available to all the parties involved in the public entity's construction project including the public entity, the architect, the construction manager, the contractors, and the first-tier and lower-tier subcontractors and shall be available for any issues arising out of the contract or construction process. The public entity may set a reasonable threshold, not to exceed fifteen thousand dollars ($15,000), concerning the amount in controversy that must be at issue before a party may require other parties to participate in the dispute resolution process. The public entity may require that the costs of the process be divided between the parties to the dispute with at least one-third of the cost to be paid by the public entity, if the public entity is a party to the dispute. The public entity may require in its contracts that a party participate in mediation concerning a dispute as a precondition to initiating litigation concerning the dispute.

(g)   Exceptions. - This section shall not apply to:

(1)   The purchase and erection of prefabricated or relocatable buildings or portions thereof, except that portion of the work which must be performed at the construction site.

(2)   The erection, construction, alteration, or repair of a building when the cost thereof is three hundred thousand dollars ($300,000) or less.

(3)   The erection, construction, alteration, or repair of a building by The University of North Carolina or its constituent institutions when the cost thereof is five hundred thousand dollars ($500,000) or less.

Notwithstanding the other provisions of this subsection, subsection (f1) of this section shall apply to any erection, construction, alteration, or repair of a building by a public entity.

§ 143-128.1. Construction management at risk contracts.

(a)   For purposes of this section and G.S. 143-64.31:

    (1)   "Construction management services" means services provided by a construction manager, which may include preparation and coordination of bid packages, scheduling, cost control, value engineering, evaluation, preconstruction services, and construction administration.

    (2)   "Construction management at risk services" means services provided by a person, corporation, or entity that (i) provides construction management services for a project throughout the preconstruction and construction phases, (ii) who is licensed as a general contractor, and (iii) who guarantees the cost of the project.

    (3)   "Construction manager at risk" means a person, corporation, or entity that provides construction management at risk services.

    (4)   "First-tier subcontractor" means a subcontractor who contracts directly with the construction manager at risk.

(b)   The construction manager at risk shall be selected in accordance with Article 3D of this Chapter. Design services for a project shall be performed by a licensed architect or engineer. The public owner shall contract directly with the architect or engineer. The public owner shall make a good-faith effort to comply with G.S. 143-128.2, G.S. 143-128.4, and to recruit and select small business entities when selecting a construction manager at risk.

(c)   The construction manager at risk shall contract directly with the public entity for all construction; shall publicly advertise as prescribed in G.S. 143-129; and shall prequalify and accept bids from first-tier subcontractors for all construction work under this section. The construction manager at risk shall use the prequalification process determined by the public entity in accordance with G.S. 143-135.8, provided that public entity and the construction manager at risk shall jointly develop the assessment tool and criteria for that specific project, which must include the prequalification scoring values and minimum required score for prequalification on that project. The public entity shall require the construction manager at risk to submit its plan for compliance with G.S. 143-128.2 for approval by the public entity prior to soliciting bids for the project's first-tier subcontractors. A construction manager at risk and first-tier subcontractors shall make a good faith effort to comply with G.S. 143-128.2, G.S. 143-128.4, and to recruit and select small business entities. A construction manager at risk may perform a portion of the work only if (i) bidding produces no responsible, responsive bidder for that portion of the work, the lowest responsible, responsive bidder will not execute a contract for the bid portion of the work, or the subcontractor defaults and a prequalified replacement cannot be obtained in a timely manner, and (ii) the public entity approves of the construction manager at risk's performance of the work. All bids shall be opened publicly, and once they are opened, shall be public records under Chapter 132 of the General Statutes. The construction manager at risk shall act as the fiduciary of the public entity in handling and opening bids. The construction manager at risk shall award the contract to the lowest responsible, responsive bidder, taking into consideration quality, performance, the time specified in the bids for performance of the contract, the cost of construction oversight, time for completion, compliance with G.S. 143-128.2, and other factors deemed appropriate by the public entity and advertised as part of the bid solicitation. The public entity may require the selection of a different first-tier subcontractor for any portion of the work, consistent with this section, provided that the construction manager at risk is compensated for any additional cost incurred.

When contracts are awarded pursuant to this section, the public entity shall provide for a dispute resolution procedure as provided in G.S. 143-128(f1).

(d)	The construction manager at risk shall provide a performance and payment bond to the public entity in accordance with the provisions of Article 3 of Chapter 44A of the General Statutes.

(e)	Construction management at risk services may be used by the public entity only after the public entity has concluded that construction management at risk services is in the best interest of the project, and the public entity has compared the advantages and disadvantages of using the construction management at risk method for a given project in lieu of the delivery methods identified in G.S. 143-128(a1)(1) through G.S. 143-128(a1)(3). The public entity may not delegate this determination.

§ 143-128.1A. Design-build contracts.

(a)   Definitions for purposes of this section:

(1)   Design-builder. - As defined in G.S. 143-128.1B.

(2)   Governmental entity. - As defined in G.S. 143-128.1B.

(b)   A governmental entity shall establish in writing the criteria used for determining the circumstances under which the design-build method is appropriate for a project, and such criteria shall, at a minimum, address all of the following:

(1)   The extent to which the governmental entity can adequately and thoroughly define the project requirements prior to the issuance of the request for qualifications for a design-builder.

(2)   The time constraints for the delivery of the project.

(3)   The ability to ensure that a quality project can be delivered.

(4)   The capability of the governmental entity to manage and oversee the project, including the availability of experienced staff or outside consultants who are experienced with the design-build method of project delivery.

(5)   A good-faith effort to comply with G.S. 143-128.2, G.S. 143-128.4, and to recruit and select small business entities. The governmental entity shall not limit or otherwise preclude any respondent from submitting a response so long as the respondent, itself or through its proposed team, is properly licensed and qualified to perform the work defined by the public notice issued under subsection (c) of this section.

(6)   The criteria utilized by the governmental entity, including a comparison of the advantages and disadvantages of using the design-build delivery method for a given project in lieu of the delivery methods identified in subdivisions (1), (2), and (4) of G.S. 143-128(a1).

(c)   A governmental entity shall issue a public notice of the request for qualifications that includes, at a minimum, general information on each of the following:

(1)   The project site.

(2)   The project scope.

(3) The anticipated project budget.
(4) The project schedule.
(5) The criteria to be considered for selection and the weighting of the qualifications criteria.
(6) Notice of any rules, ordinances, or goals established by the governmental entity, including goals for minority- and women-owned business participation and small business participation.
(7) Other information provided by the owner to potential design-builders in submitting qualifications for the project.
(8) A statement providing that each design-builder shall submit in its response to the request for qualifications an explanation of its project team selection, which shall consist of either of the following:
    a. A list of the licensed contractors, licensed subcontractors, and licensed design professionals whom the design-builder proposes to use for the project's design and construction.
    b. An outline of the strategy the design-builder plans to use for open contractor and subcontractor selection based upon the provisions of Article 8 of Chapter 143 of the General Statutes.

(d) Following evaluation of the qualifications of the design-builders, the three most highly qualified design-builders shall be ranked. If after the solicitation for design-builders not as many as three responses have been received from qualified design-builders, the governmental entity shall again solicit for design-builders. If as a result of such second solicitation not as many as three responses are received, the governmental entity may then begin negotiations with the highest-ranked design-builder under G.S. 143-64.31 even though fewer than three responses were received. If the governmental entity deems it appropriate, the governmental entity may invite some or all responders to interview with the governmental entity.

(e) The design-builder shall be selected in accordance with Article 3D of this Chapter. Each design-builder shall certify to the governmental entity that each licensed design professional who is a member of the design-build team, including subconsultants, was selected based upon demonstrated competence and qualifications in the manner provided by G.S. 143-64.31.

(f)   The design-builder shall provide a performance and payment bond to the governmental entity in accordance with the provisions of Article 3 of Chapter 44A of the General Statutes. The design-builder shall obtain written approval from the governmental entity prior to changing key personnel as listed in sub-subdivision (c)(8)a. of this section after the contract has been awarded.

§ 143-128.1B. Design-build bridging contracts.

(a)   Definitions for purposes of this section:

(1)   Design-build bridging. - A design and construction delivery process whereby a governmental entity contracts for design criteria services under a separate agreement from the construction phase services of the design-builder.

(2)   Design-builder. - An appropriately licensed person, corporation, or entity that, under a single contract, offers to provide or provides design services and general contracting services where services within the scope of the practice of professional engineering or architecture are performed respectively by a licensed engineer or licensed architect and where services within the scope of the practice of general contracting are performed by a licensed general contractor.

(3)   Design criteria. - The requirements for a public project expressed in drawings and specifications sufficient to allow the design-builder to make a responsive bid proposal.

(4)   Design professional. - Any professional licensed under Chapters 83A, 89A, or 89C of the General Statutes.

(5)   First-tier subcontractor. - A subcontractor who contracts directly with the design-builder, excluding design professionals.

(6)   Governmental entity. - Every officer, board, department, commission, or commissions charged with responsibility of preparation of specifications or awarding or entering into contracts for the erection, construction, alteration, or repair of any buildings for the State or for any county, municipality, or other public body.

(b)   A governmental entity shall establish in writing the criteria used for determining the circumstances under which engaging a design criteria design professional is appropriate for a project, and such criteria shall, at a minimum, address all of the following:

(1)   The extent to which the governmental entity can adequately and thoroughly define the project requirements prior to the issuance of the request for proposals for a design-builder.

(2)   The time constraints for the delivery of the project.

(3)   The ability to ensure that a quality project can be delivered.

(4)   The capability of the governmental entity to manage and oversee the project, including the availability of experienced staff or outside consultants who are experienced with the design-build method of project delivery.

(5)   A good-faith effort to comply with G.S. 143-128.2, G.S. 143-128.4, and to recruit and select small business entities. The governmental entity shall not limit or otherwise preclude any respondent from submitting a response so long as the respondent, itself or through its proposed team, is properly licensed and qualified to perform the work defined by the public notice issued under subsection (d) of this section.

(6)   The criteria utilized by the governmental entity, including a comparison of the advantages and disadvantages of using the design-build delivery method for a given project in lieu of the delivery methods identified in subdivisions (1), (2), and (4) of G.S. 143-128(a1).

(c)   On or before entering into a contract for design-build services under this section, the governmental entity shall select or designate a staff design professional, or a design professional who is independent of the design-builder, to act as its design criteria design professional as its representative for the procurement process and for the duration of the design and construction. If the design professional is not a full-time employee of the governmental entity, the governmental entity shall select the design professional on the basis of demonstrated competence and qualifications as provided by G.S. 143-64.31. The design criteria design professional shall develop design criteria in consultation with the governmental entity. The design criteria design professional shall not be eligible to submit a response to the request for proposals nor provide design input to a design-build response to the request for proposals. The design criteria design professional shall prepare a design criteria package equal to thirty-five percent (35%) of the completed design documentation for the entire construction project. The design criteria package shall include all of the following:

    (1)   Programmatic needs, interior space requirements, intended space utilization, and other capacity requirements.

    (2)   Information on the physical characteristics of the site, such as a topographic survey.

    (3)   Material quality standards or performance criteria.

    (4)   Special material requirements.

    (5)   Provisions for utilities.

    (6)   Parking requirements.

    (7)   The type, size, and location of adjacent structures.

    (8)   Preliminary or conceptual drawings and specifications sufficient in detail to allow the design-builder to make a proposal which is responsive to the request for proposals.

    (9)   Notice of any ordinances, rules, or goals adopted by the governmental entity.

  (d)   A governmental entity shall issue a public notice of the request for proposals that includes, at a minimum, general information on each of the following:

    (1)   The project site.

    (2)   The project scope.

    (3)   The anticipated project budget.

    (4)   The project schedule.

    (5)   The criteria to be considered for selection and the weighting of the selection criteria.

    (6)   Notice of any rules, ordinances, or goals established by the governmental entity, including goals for minority- and women-owned business participation and small business entities.

    (7)   The thirty-five percent (35%) design criteria package prepared by the design criteria design professional.

    (8)   Other information provided by the owner to design-builders in submitting responses to the request for proposals for the project.

    (9)   A statement providing that each design-builder shall submit in its request for proposal response an explanation of

its project team selection, which shall consist of a list of the licensed contractor and licensed design professionals whom the design-builder proposes to use for the project's design and construction.

(10) A statement providing that each design-builder shall submit in its request for proposal a sealed envelope with all of the following:

    a. The design-builder's price for providing the general conditions of the contract.

    b. The design-builder's proposed fee for general construction services.

    c. The design-builder's fee for design services.

(e) Following evaluation of the qualifications of the design-builders, the governmental entity shall rank the design-builders who have provided responses, grouping the top three without ordinal ranking. If after the solicitation for design-builders not as many as three responses have been received from qualified design-builders, the governmental entity shall again solicit for design-builders. If as a result of such second solicitation not as many as three responses are received, the governmental entity may then make its selection. From the grouping of the top three design-builders, the governmental entity shall select the design-builder who is the lowest responsive, responsible bidder based on the cumulative amount of fees provided in accordance with subdivision (d)(10) of this section and taking into consideration quality, performance, and the time specified in the proposals for the performance of the contract. Each design-builder shall certify to the governmental entity that each licensed design professional who is a member of the design-build team, including subconsultants, was selected based upon demonstrated competence and qualifications in the manner provided by G.S. 143-64.31.

(f) The design-builder shall accept bids based upon the provisions of this Article from first-tier subcontractors for all construction work under this section.

(g) The design-builder shall provide a performance and payment bond to the governmental entity in accordance with the provisions of Article 3 of Chapter 44A of the General Statutes. The design-builder shall obtain written approval from the governmental entity prior to changing key personnel, as listed under subdivision (d)(9) of this section, after the contract has been awarded.

§ 143-128.1C. Public-private partnership construction contracts.

(a) Definitions for purposes of this section:

(1) Construction contract. - Any contract entered into between a private developer and a contractor for the design, construction, reconstruction, alteration, or repair of any building or other work or improvement required for a private developer to satisfy its obligations under a development contract.

(2) Contractor. - Any person who has entered into a construction contract with a private developer under this section.

(3) Design-builder. - Defined in G.S. 143-128.1B.

(4) Development contract. - Any contract between a governmental entity and a private developer under this section and, as part of the contract, the private developer is required to provide at least fifty percent (50%) of the financing for the total cost necessary to deliver the capital improvement project, whether through lease or ownership, for the governmental entity.

(5) Governmental entity. - Defined in G.S. 143-128.1B.

(6) Labor or materials. - Includes all materials furnished or labor performed in the performance of the work required by a construction contract whether or not the labor or materials enter into or become a component part of the improvement and shall include gas, power, light, heat, oil, gasoline, telephone services, and rental of equipment or the reasonable value of the use of equipment directly utilized in the performance of the work required by a construction contract.

(7) Private developer. - Any person who has entered into a development contract with a governmental entity under this section.

(8) Public-private project. - A capital improvement project undertaken for the benefit of a governmental entity and a private developer pursuant to a development contract that includes construction of a public facility or other improvements, including paving, grading, utilities, infrastructure, reconstruction, or repair, and may include both public and private facilities.

(9) State entity. - The State and every agency, authority, institution, board, commission, bureau, council, department, division, officer, or employee of the State. The term does not include a unit of local government as defined in G.S. 159-7.

(10) State-supported financing arrangement. - Any installment financing arrangement, lease-purchase arrangement, arrangement under which funds are to be paid in the future based upon the availability of an asset or funds for payment, or any similar arrangement in the nature of a financing, under which a State entity agrees to make payments to acquire or obtain a capital asset for the State entity or any other State entity for a term, including renewal options, of greater than one year. Any arrangement that results in the identification of a portion of a lease payment, installment payment, or similar scheduled payment thereunder by a State entity as "interest" for purposes of federal income taxation shall automatically be a State-supported financing arrangement for purposes of this section.

(11) Subcontractor. - Any person who has contracted to furnish labor, services, or materials to, or who has performed labor or services for, a contractor or another subcontractor in connection with a development contract.

(b) If the governmental entity determines in writing that it has a critical need for a capital improvement project, the governmental entity may acquire, construct, own, lease as lessor or lessee, and operate or participate in the acquisition, construction, ownership, leasing, and operation of a public-private project, or of specific facilities within such a project, including the making of loans and grants from funds available to the governmental entity for these purposes. If the governmental entity is a public body under Article 33C of this Chapter, the determination shall occur during an open meeting of that public body. The governmental entity may enter into development contracts with private developers with respect to acquiring, constructing, owning, leasing, or operating a project under this section. The development contract shall specify the following:

(1) The property interest of the governmental entity and all other participants in the development of the project.

    (2)   The responsibilities of the governmental entity and all other participants in the development of the project.

    (3)   The responsibilities of the governmental entity and all other participants with respect to financing of the project.

    (4)   The responsibilities to put forth a good-faith effort to comply with G.S. 143-128.2, G.S. 143-128.4, and to recruit and select small business entities.

(c)   The development contract may provide that the private developer shall be responsible for any or all of the following:

    (1)   Construction of the entire public-private project.

    (2)   Reconstruction or repair of the public-private project or any part thereof subsequent to construction of the project.

    (3)   Construction of any addition to the public-private project.

    (4)   Renovation of the public-private project or any part thereof.

    (5)   Purchase of apparatus, supplies, materials, or equipment for the public-private project whether during or subsequent to the initial equipping of the project.

    (6)   A good-faith effort to comply with G.S. 143-128.2, G.S. 143-128.4, and to recruit and select small business entities.

(d)   The development contract may also provide that the governmental entity and private developer shall use the same contractor or contractors in constructing a portion of or the entire public-private project. If the development contract provides that the governmental entity and private developer shall use the same contractor, the development contract shall include provisions deemed appropriate by the governmental entity to assure that the public facility or facilities included in or added to the public-private project are constructed, reconstructed, repaired, or renovated at a reasonable price and that the apparatus, supplies, materials, and equipment purchased for the public facility or facilities included in the public-private project are purchased at a reasonable price. For public-private partnerships using the design-build project delivery method, the provisions of G.S. 143-128.1A shall apply.

(e)   A private developer and its contractors shall make a good-faith effort to comply with G.S. 143-128.2, G.S. 143-128.4, and to recruit and select small business entities.

(f)   A private developer may perform a portion of the construction or design work only if both of the following criteria apply:

    (1)   A previously engaged contractor defaults, and a qualified replacement cannot be obtained after a good-faith effort has been made in a timely manner.

    (2)   The governmental entity approves the private developer to perform the work.

(g)   The following bonding provisions apply to any development contract entered into under this section:

    (1)   A payment bond shall be required for any development contract as follows: A payment bond in the amount of one hundred percent (100%) of the total anticipated amount of the construction contracts to be entered into between the private developer and the contractors to design or construct the improvements required by the development contract. The payment bond shall be conditioned upon the prompt payment for all labor or materials for which the private developer or one or more of its contractors or those contractors' subcontractors are liable. The payment bond shall be solely for the protection of the persons furnishing materials or performing labor or services for which the private developer or its contractors or subcontractors are liable. The total anticipated amount of the construction contracts shall be stated in the development contract and certified by the private developer as being a good-faith projection of its total costs for designing and constructing the improvements required by the development contract. The payment bond shall be executed by one or more surety companies legally authorized to do business in the State of North Carolina and shall become effective upon the awarding of the development contract. The development contract may provide for the requirement of a performance bond.

    (2)   a.   Subject to the provisions of this subsection, any claimant who has performed labor or furnished materials in the prosecution of the work required by any contract for which a payment bond has been given pursuant to the provisions of this subsection, and who has not been

paid in full therefor before the expiration of 90 days after the day on which the claimant performed the last labor or furnished the last materials for which that claimant claims payment, may bring an action on the payment bond in that claimant's own name to recover any amount due to that claimant for the labor or materials and may prosecute the action to final judgment and have execution on the judgment.

b. Any claimant who has a direct contractual relationship with any contractor or any subcontractor but has no contractual relationship, express or implied, with the private developer may bring an action on the payment bond only if that claimant has given written notice of claim on the payment bond to the private developer within 120 days from the date on which the claimant performed the last of the labor or furnished the last of the materials for which that claimant claims payment, in which that claimant states with substantial accuracy the amount claimed and the name of the person for whom the work was performed or to whom the material was furnished.

c. The notice required by sub-subdivision b. of this subdivision shall be served by certified mail or by signature confirmation as provided by the United States Postal Service, postage prepaid, in an envelope addressed to the private developer at any place where that private developer's office is regularly maintained for the transaction of business or in any manner provided by law for the service of summons. The claimants' service of a claim of lien on real property or a claim of lien on funds as funds as allowed by Article 2 of Chapter 44A of the General Statutes on the private developer shall be deemed, nonexclusively, as adequate notice under this section.

(3) Every action on a payment bond as provided in this subsection shall be brought in a court of appropriate jurisdiction in a county where the development contract or any part

thereof is to be or has been performed. Except as provided in G.S. 44A-16(c), no action on a payment bond shall be commenced after one year from the day on which the last of the labor was performed or material was furnished by the claimant.

(4)   No surety shall be liable under a payment bond for a total amount greater than the face amount of the payment bond. A judgment against any surety may be reduced or set aside upon motion by the surety and a showing that the total amount of claims paid and judgments previously rendered under the payment bond, together with the amount of the judgment to be reduced or set aside, exceeds the face amount of the bond.

(5)   No act of or agreement between the governmental entity, a private developer, or a surety shall reduce the period of time for giving notice under sub-subdivision (2)b. of this subsection or commencing action under subdivision (3) of this subsection or otherwise reduce or limit the liability of the private developer or surety as prescribed in this subsection. Every bond given by a private developer pursuant to this subsection shall be conclusively presumed to have been given in accordance with the provisions of this subsection, whether or not the bond is drawn as to conform to this subsection. The provisions of this subsection shall be conclusively presumed to have been written into every bond given pursuant to this subsection.

(6)   Any person entitled to bring an action or any defendant in an action on a payment bond shall have a right to require the governmental entity or the private developer to certify and furnish a copy of the payment bond, the development contract, and any construction contracts covered by the bond. It shall be the duty of the private developer or the governmental entity to give any such person a certified copy of the payment bond and the construction contract upon not less than 10 days' notice and request. The governmental entity or private developer may require a reasonable payment for the actual cost of furnishing the certified copy. A copy of any

payment bond, development contract, and any construction contracts covered by the bond certified by the governmental entity or private developer shall constitute prima facie evidence of the contents, execution, and delivery of the bond, development contract, and construction contracts.

(7) A payment bond form containing the following provisions shall comply with this subsection:

a. The date the bond is executed.

b. The name of the principal.

c. The name of the surety.

d. The governmental entity.

e. The development contract number.

f. All of the following:

1. "KNOW ALL MEN BY THESE PRESENTS, That we, the PRINCIPAL and SURETY above named, are held and firmly bound unto the above named [governmental entity], hereinafter called [governmental entity], in the penal sum of the amount stated above, for the payment of which sum well and truly to be made, we bind ourselves, our heirs, executors, administrators, and successors, jointly and severally, firmly by these presents."

2. "THE CONDITION OF THIS OBLIGATION IS SUCH, that whereas the Principal entered into a certain development contract with [governmental entity], numbered as shown above and hereto attached."

3. "NOW THEREFORE, if the Principal shall promptly make payment to all persons supplying labor and material in the prosecution of the construction or design work provided for in the development contract, and any and all duly authorized modifications of the contract that may hereafter be made, notice of which modifications to the surety being hereby waived, then this obligation to be void; otherwise to remain in full force and virtue."

4. "IN WITNESS WHEREOF, the above bounden parties have executed this instrument under their several seals on the date indicated above, the name and corporate seal of each corporate party being hereto affixed and these presents duly signed by its undersigned representative, pursuant to authority of its governing body." Appropriate places for execution by the surety and principal shall be provided.

(8) In any suit brought or defended under the provisions of this subsection, the presiding judge may allow reasonable attorneys' fees to the attorney representing the prevailing party. Attorneys' fees under this subdivision are to be taxed as part of the court costs and shall be payable by the losing party upon a finding that there was an unreasonable refusal by the losing party to fully resolve the matter which constituted the basis of the suit or the basis of the defense. For purposes of this subdivision, the term "prevailing party" means a party plaintiff or third-party plaintiff who obtains a judgment of at least fifty percent (50%) of the monetary amount sought in a claim or a party defendant or third-party defendant against whom a claim is asserted which results in a judgment of less than fifty percent (50%) of the amount sought in the claim defended. Notwithstanding the provisions of this subdivision, if an offer of judgment is served in accordance with G.S. 1A-1, Rule 68, a "prevailing party" is an offeree who obtains judgment in an amount more favorable than the last offer or is an offeror against whom judgment is rendered in an amount less favorable than the last offer.

(9) The obligations and lien rights set forth in Article 2 of Chapter 44A of the General Statutes shall apply to a project awarded under this section to the extent of any property interests held by the private developer in the project. For purposes of applying the provisions of Article 2 of Chapter 44A of the General Statutes, the private developer shall be deemed the owner to the extent of that private developer's ownership interest. This subdivision shall not be construed

as making the provisions of Article 2 of Chapter 44A of the General Statutes apply to governmental entities or public buildings to the extent of any property interest held by the governmental entity in the building.

(h) The governmental entity shall determine its programming requirements for facilities to be constructed under this section and shall determine the form in which private developers may submit their qualifications. The governmental entity shall advertise a notice for interested private developers to submit qualifications in a newspaper having general circulation within the county in which the governmental entity is located. Prior to the submission of qualifications, the governmental entity shall make available, in whatever form it deems appropriate, the programming requirements for facilities included in the public-private project. Any private developer submitting qualifications shall include the following:

(1) Evidence of financial stability. However, "trade secrets" as that term is defined in G.S. 66-152(3) shall be exempt from disclosure under Chapter 132 of the General Statutes.

(2) Experience with similar projects.

(3) Explanation of project team selection by either listing of licensed contractors, licensed subcontractors, and licensed design professionals whom the private developer proposes to use for the project's design and construction or a statement outlining a strategy for open contractor and subcontractor selection based upon the provisions of this Article.

(4) Statement of availability to undertake the public-private project and projected time line for project completion.

(5) Any other information required by the governmental entity.

(i) Based upon the qualifications package submitted by the private developers and any other information required by the governmental entity, the governmental entity may select one or more private developers with whom to negotiate the terms and conditions of a contract to perform the public-private project. The governmental entity shall advertise the terms of the proposed contract to be entered into by the governmental entity in a newspaper having general circulation within the county in which the governmental entity is located at least 30 days prior to entering into the development contract. If the governmental entity is a public body under Article 33C of this Chapter, the development contract shall be considered in an open meeting of that public body following a public hearing on the proposed development contract. Notice of the public hearing shall be published in the same notice as the advertisement of the terms under this subsection.

(j)   The governmental entity shall make available a summary of the development contract terms which shall include a statement of how to obtain a copy of the complete development contract.

(k)   Leases entered into under this section are subject to approval as follows:

(1)   If a capital lease or operating lease is entered into by a unit of local government as defined in G.S. 159-7, that capital lease or operating lease is subject to approval by the local government commission under Article 8 of Chapter 159 of the General Statutes if it meets the standards set out in G.S. 159-148(a)(1), 159-148(a)(2), and 159-148(a)(3), 159-148(a)(4) or 159-153. For purposes of determining whether the standards set out in G.S. 159-148(a)(3) have been met, only the five hundred thousand dollar ($500,000) threshold applies.

(2)   If a capital lease is entered into by a State entity that constitutes a State-supported financing arrangement and requires payments thereunder that are payable, whether directly or indirectly, and whether or not subject to the appropriation of funds for such payment, by payments from the General Fund of the State or other funds and accounts of the State that are funded from the general revenues and other taxes and fees of the State or State entities, not including taxes and fees that are required to be deposited to the Highway Fund or Highway Trust Fund, that capital lease shall be subject to the approval procedures required for special indebtedness by G.S. 142-83 and G.S. 142-84. This requirement shall not apply to any arrangement where bonds or other obligations are issued or incurred by a State entity to carry out a financing program authorized by the General Assembly under which such bonds or other obligations are payable from monies derived from specified, limited, nontax sources, so long as the payments under that arrangement by a State

entity are limited to the sources authorized by the General Assembly.

(l)   A capital lease or operating lease entered into under this section may not contain any provision with respect to the assignment of specific students or students from a specific area to any specific school.

(m)   This section shall not apply to any contract or other agreement between or among The University of North Carolina or one of its constituent institutions, a private, nonprofit corporation established under Part 2B of Article 1 of Chapter 116 of the General Statutes, or any private foundation, private association, or private club created for the primary purpose of financial support to The University of North Carolina or one of its constituent institutions.

§ 143-128.2. Minority business participation goals.

(a)   The State shall have a verifiable ten percent (10%) goal for participation by minority businesses in the total value of work for each State building project, including building projects done by a private entity on a facility to be leased or purchased by the State. A local government unit or other public or private entity that receives State appropriations for a building project or other State grant funds for a building project, including a building project done by a private entity on a facility to be leased or purchased by the local government unit, where the project cost is one hundred thousand dollars ($100,000) or more, shall have a verifiable ten percent (10%) goal for participation by minority businesses in the total value of the work; provided, however, a local government unit may apply a different verifiable goal that was adopted prior to December 1, 2001, if the local government unit had and continues to have a sufficiently strong basis in evidence to justify the use of that goal. On State building projects and building projects subject to the State goal requirement, the Secretary shall identify the appropriate percentage goal, based on adequate data, for each category of minority business as defined in G.S. 143-128.2(g)(1) based on the specific contract type.

Except as otherwise provided for in this subsection, each city, county, or other local public entity shall adopt, after a notice and public hearing, an appropriate verifiable percentage goal for participation by minority businesses in the total value of work for building projects.

Each entity required to have verifiable percentage goals under this subsection shall make a good faith effort to recruit minority participation in accordance with this section or G.S. 143-131(b), as applicable.

(b)   A public entity shall establish prior to solicitation of bids the good faith efforts that it will take to make it feasible for minority businesses to submit successful bids or proposals for the contracts for building projects. Public entities shall make good faith efforts as set forth in subsection (e) of this section. Public entities shall require contractors to make good faith efforts pursuant to subsection (f) of this section. Each first-tier subcontractor on a construction management at risk project shall comply with the requirements applicable to contractors under this subsection.

(c)   Each bidder, which shall mean first-tier subcontractor for construction manager at risk projects for purposes of this subsection, on a project bid under any of the methods authorized under G.S. 143-128(a1) shall identify on its bid the minority businesses that it will use on the project and an affidavit listing the good faith efforts it has made pursuant to subsection (f) of this section and the total dollar value of the bid that will be performed by the minority businesses. A contractor, including a first-tier subcontractor on a construction manager at risk project, that performs all of the work under a contract with its own workforce may submit an affidavit to that effect in lieu of the affidavit otherwise required under this subsection. The apparent lowest responsible, responsive bidder shall also file the following:

(1)   Within the time specified in the bid documents, either:

a.   An affidavit that includes a description of the portion of work to be executed by minority businesses, expressed as a percentage of the total contract price, which is equal to or more than the applicable goal. An affidavit under this sub-subdivision shall give rise to a presumption that the bidder has made the required good faith or effort; or

b.   Documentation of its good faith effort to meet the goal. The documentation must include evidence of all good faith efforts that were implemented, including any advertisements, solicitations, and evidence of other specific actions demonstrating recruitment and selection of minority businesses for participation in the contract.

(2)   Within 30 days after award of the contract, a list of all identified subcontractors that the contractor will use on the project.

Failure to file a required affidavit or documentation that demonstrates that the contractor made the required good faith effort is grounds for rejection of the bid.

(d)   No subcontractor who is identified and listed pursuant to subsection (c) of this section may be replaced with a different subcontractor except:

(1)   If the subcontractor's bid is later determined by the contractor or construction manager at risk to be nonresponsible or nonresponsive, or the listed subcontractor refuses to enter into a contract for the complete performance of the bid work, or

(2)   With the approval of the public entity for good cause.

Good faith efforts as set forth in G.S. 143-131(b) shall apply to the selection of a substitute subcontractor. Prior to substituting a subcontractor, the contractor shall identify the substitute subcontractor and inform the public entity of its good faith efforts pursuant to G.S. 143-131(b).

(e)   Before awarding a contract, a public entity shall do the following:

(1)   Develop and implement a minority business participation outreach plan to identify minority businesses that can perform public building projects and to implement outreach efforts to encourage minority business participation in these projects to include education, recruitment, and interaction between minority businesses and nonminority businesses.

(2)   Attend the scheduled prebid conference.

(3)   At least 10 days prior to the scheduled day of bid opening, notify minority businesses that have requested notices from the public entity for public construction or repair work and minority businesses that otherwise indicated to the Office of Historically Underutilized Businesses an interest in the type of work being bid or the potential contracting opportunities listed in the proposal. The notification shall include the following:

    a.   A description of the work for which the bid is being solicited.

    b.   The date, time, and location where bids are to be submitted.

    c.   The name of the individual within the public entity who will be available to answer questions about the project.

    d.   Where bid documents may be reviewed.

    e.   Any special requirements that may exist.

(4)   Utilize other media, as appropriate, likely to inform potential minority businesses of the bid being sought.

(f)   A public entity shall require bidders to undertake the following good faith efforts to the extent required by the Secretary on projects subject to this section. The Secretary shall adopt rules establishing points to be awarded for taking each effort and the minimum number of points required, depending on project size, cost, type, and other factors considered relevant by the Secretary. In establishing the point system, the Secretary may not require a contractor to earn more than fifty (50) points, and the Secretary must assign each of the efforts listed in subdivisions (1) through (10) of this subsection at least 10 points. The public entity may require that additional good faith efforts be taken, as indicated in its bid specifications. Good faith efforts include:

(1)   Contacting minority businesses that reasonably could have been expected to submit a quote and that were known to the contractor or available on State or local government maintained lists at least 10 days before the bid or proposal date and notifying them of the nature and scope of the work to be performed.

(2)   Making the construction plans, specifications and requirements available for review by prospective minority businesses, or providing these documents to them at least 10 days before the bid or proposals are due.

(3)   Breaking down or combining elements of work into economically feasible units to facilitate minority participation.

(4)   Working with minority trade, community, or contractor organizations identified by the Office of Historically Underutilized Businesses and included in the bid documents that provide assistance in recruitment of minority businesses.

(5) Attending any prebid meetings scheduled by the public owner.

(6) Providing assistance in getting required bonding or insurance or providing alternatives to bonding or insurance for subcontractors.

(7) Negotiating in good faith with interested minority businesses and not rejecting them as unqualified without sound reasons based on their capabilities. Any rejection of a minority business based on lack of qualification should have the reasons documented in writing.

(8) Providing assistance to an otherwise qualified minority business in need of equipment, loan capital, lines of credit, or joint pay agreements to secure loans, supplies, or letters of credit, including waiving credit that is ordinarily required. Assisting minority businesses in obtaining the same unit pricing with the bidder's suppliers in order to help minority businesses in establishing credit.

(9) Negotiating joint venture and partnership arrangements with minority businesses in order to increase opportunities for minority business participation on a public construction or repair project when possible.

(10) Providing quick pay agreements and policies to enable minority contractors and suppliers to meet cash-flow demands.

(g) As used in this section:

(1) The term "minority business" means a business:

a. In which at least fifty-one percent (51%) is owned by one or more minority persons or socially and economically disadvantaged individuals, or in the case of a corporation, in which at least fifty-one percent (51%) of the stock is owned by one or more minority persons or socially and economically disadvantaged individuals; and

b. Of which the management and daily business operations are controlled by one or more of the minority persons or socially and economically disadvantaged individuals who own it.

(2) The term "minority person" means a person who is a citizen or lawful permanent resident of the United States and who is:

    a. Black, that is, a person having origins in any of the black racial groups in Africa;

    b. Hispanic, that is, a person of Spanish or Portuguese culture with origins in Mexico, South or Central America, or the Caribbean Islands, regardless of race;

    c. Asian American, that is, a person having origins in any of the original peoples of the Far East, Southeast Asia and Asia, the Indian subcontinent, or the Pacific Islands;

    d. American Indian, that is, a person having origins in any of the original Indian peoples of North America; or

    e. Female.

(3) The term "socially and economically disadvantaged individual" means the same as defined in 15 U.S.C. [§] 637.

(h) The State, counties, municipalities, and all other public bodies shall award public building contracts, including those awarded under G.S. 143-128.1, 143-129, and 143-131, without regard to race, religion, color, creed, national origin, sex, age, or handicapping condition, as defined in G.S. 168A-3. Nothing in this section shall be construed to require contractors or awarding authorities to award contracts or subcontracts to or to make purchases of materials or equipment from minority-business contractors or minority-business subcontractors who do not submit the lowest responsible, responsive bid or bids.

(i) Notwithstanding G.S. 132-3 and G.S. 121-5, all public records created pursuant to this section shall be maintained by the public entity for a period of not less than three years from the date of the completion of the building project.

(j) Except as provided in subsections (a), (g), (h) and (i) of this section, this section shall only apply to building projects costing three hundred thousand dollars ($300,000) or more. This section shall not apply to the purchase and erection of prefabricated or relocatable buildings or portions thereof, except that portion of the work which must be performed at the construction site.

§ 143-128.3. Minority business participation administration.

(a) All public entities subject to G.S. 143-128.2 shall report to the Department of Administration, Office of Historically Underutilized Business, the following with respect to each building project:

(1) The verifiable percentage goal.

(2) The type and total dollar value of the project, minority business utilization by minority business category, trade, total dollar value of contracts awarded to each minority group for each project, the applicable good faith effort guidelines or rules used to recruit minority business participation, and good faith documentation accepted by the public entity from the successful bidder.

(3) The utilization of minority businesses under the various construction methods under G.S. 143-128(a1).

The reports shall be in the format and contain the data prescribed by the Secretary of Administration. The University of North Carolina and the State Board of Community Colleges shall report quarterly and all other public entities shall report semiannually. The Secretary of the Department of Administration shall make reports every six months to the Joint Legislative Committee on Governmental Operations on information reported pursuant to this subsection.

(b) A public entity that has been notified by the Secretary of its failure to comply with G.S. 143-128.2 on a project shall develop a plan of compliance that addresses the deficiencies identified by the Secretary. The corrective plan shall apply to the current project or to subsequent projects under G.S. 143-128, as appropriate, provided that the plan must be implemented, at a minimum, on the current project to the extent feasible. If the public entity, after notification from the Secretary, fails to file a corrective plan, or if the public entity does not implement the corrective plan in accordance with its terms, the Secretary shall require one or both of the following:

(1) That the public entity consult with the Department of Administration, Office of Historically Underutilized Businesses on the development of a new corrective plan, subject to the approval of the Department and the Attorney General. The public entity may designate a representative to appear on its behalf, provided that the representative has managerial responsibility for the construction project.

(2) That the public entity not bid another contract under G.S. 143-128 without prior review by the Department and the Attorney General of a good faith compliance plan developed pursuant to subdivision (1) of this subsection. The public entity shall be subject to the review and approval of its good faith compliance plan under this subdivision with respect to any projects bid pursuant to G.S. 143-128 during a period of time determined by the Secretary, not to exceed one year.

A public entity aggrieved by the decision of the Secretary may file a contested case proceeding under Chapter 150B of the General Statutes.

(c) The Secretary shall study and recommend to the General Assembly and other State agencies ways to improve the effectiveness and efficiency of the State capital facilities development, minority business participation program and good faith efforts in utilizing minority businesses as set forth in G.S. 143-128.2, and other appropriate good faith efforts that may result in the increased utilization of minority businesses.

(d) The Secretary shall appoint an advisory board to develop recommendations to improve the recruitment and utilization of minority businesses. The Secretary, with the input of its advisory board, shall review the State's programs for promoting the recruitment and utilization of minority businesses involved in State capital projects and shall recommend to the General Assembly, the State Construction Office, The University of North Carolina, and the community colleges system changes in the terms and conditions of State laws, rules, and policies that will enhance opportunities for utilization of minority businesses on these projects. The Secretary shall provide guidance to these agencies on identifying types of projects likely to attract increased participation by minority businesses and breaking down or combining elements of work into economically feasible units to facilitate minority business participation.

(e) The Secretary shall adopt rules for State entities, The University of North Carolina, and community colleges and shall adopt guidelines for local government units to implement the provisions of G.S. 143-128.2.

(e1) Repealed by Session Laws 2007-392, s. 3, effective October 1, 2007.

(f) The Secretary shall provide the following information to the Attorney General:

(1) Failure by a public entity to report data to the Secretary in accordance with this section.

(2) Upon the request of the Attorney General, any data or other information collected under this section.

(3) False statements knowingly provided in any affidavit or documentation under G.S. 143-128.2 to the State or other public entity. Public entities shall provide to the Secretary information concerning any false information knowingly provided to the public entity pursuant to G.S. 143-128.2.

(g) The Secretary shall report findings and recommendations as required under this section to the Joint Legislative Committee on Governmental Operations annually on or before June 1, beginning June 1, 2002.

§ 143-128.4. Historically underutilized business defined; statewide uniform certification.

(a) As used in this Chapter, the term "historically underutilized business" means a business that meets all of the following conditions:

(1) At least fifty-one percent (51%) of the business is owned by one or more persons who are members of at least one of the groups set forth in subsection (b) of this section, or in the case of a corporation, at least fifty-one percent (51%) of the stock is owned by one or more persons who are members of at least one of the groups set forth in subsection (b) of this section.

(2) The management and daily business operations are controlled by one or more owners of the business who are members of at least one of the groups set forth in subsection (b) of this section.

(a1) As used in this Chapter, the term "minority business" means a historically underutilized business.

(b) To qualify as a historically underutilized business under this section, a business must be owned and controlled as set forth in subsection (a) of this section by one or more citizens or lawful permanent residents of the United States who are members of one or more of the following groups:

(1) Black. - A person having origins in any of the black racial groups of Africa.

(2) Hispanic. - A person of Spanish or Portuguese culture having origins in Mexico, South or Central America, or the Caribbean islands, regardless of race.

(3)   Asian American. - A person having origins in any of the
       original peoples of the Far East, Southeast Asia, Asia, Indian
       continent, or Pacific islands.
(4)   American Indian. - A person having origins in any of the
       original Indian peoples of North America.
(5)   Female.
(6)   Disabled. - A person with a disability as defined in G.S. 168-1
       or G.S. 168A-3.
(7)   Disadvantaged. - A person who is socially and economically
       disadvantaged as defined in 15 U.S.C. § 637.

(c)   In addition to the powers and duties provided in G.S. 143-49, the
Secretary of Administration shall have the power, authority, and duty to:

(1)   Develop and administer a statewide uniform program for: (i)
       the certification of a historically underutilized business, as
       defined in this section, for use by State departments, agen-
       cies, and institutions, and political subdivisions of the State;
       and (ii) the creation and maintenance of a database of the
       businesses certified as historically underutilized businesses.
(2)   Adopt rules and procedures for the statewide uniform certi-
       fication of historically underutilized businesses.
(3)   Provide for the certification of all businesses designated as
       historically underutilized businesses to be used by State
       departments, agencies, and institutions, and political subdi-
       visions of the State.

(d)   The Secretary of Administration shall seek input from State
departments, agencies, and institutions, political subdivisions of the State,
and any other entity deemed appropriate to determine the qualifications
and criteria for statewide uniform certification of historically underutilized
businesses.

(e)   Only businesses certified in accordance with this section shall be
considered by State departments, agencies, and institutions, and political subdivisions of the State as historically underutilized businesses for
minority business participation purposes under this Chapter.

§ 143-129.2. Construction, design, and operation of solid waste management and sludge management facilities.

(a)   All terms relating to solid waste management and disposal as used in this section shall be defined as set forth in G.S. 130A-290, except that the term "unit of local government" also includes a sanitary district created under Part 2 of Article 2 of Chapter 130A of the General Statutes, an authority created under Article 1 of Chapter 162A of the General Statutes, a metropolitan sewerage district created under Article 5 of Chapter 162A of the General Statutes, and a county water and sewer district created under Article 6 of Chapter 162A of the General Statutes. As used in this section, the term "sludge management facility" means a facility that processes sludge that has been generated by a municipal wastewater treatment plant for final end use or disposal but does not include any component of a wastewater treatment process or facility that generates sludge.

(b)   To acknowledge the highly complex and innovative nature of solid waste and sludge management technologies for processing mixed solid waste and sludge generated by water and wastewater treatment facilities, the relatively limited availability of existing and proven proprietary technology involving solid waste and sludge management facilities, the desirability of a single point of responsibility for the development of facilities and the economic and technical utility of contracts for solid waste and sludge management which include in their scope combinations of design, construction, operation, management and maintenance responsibilities over prolonged periods of time and that in some instances it may be beneficial to a unit of local government to award a contract on the basis of factors other than cost alone, including but not limited to facility design, operational experience, system reliability, energy production efficiency, long-term operational costs, compatibility with source separation and other recycling systems, environmental impact and operational guarantees. Accordingly, and notwithstanding other provisions of this Article or any local law, a contract entered into between a unit of local government and any person pursuant to this section may be awarded in accordance with the following provisions for the award of a contract based upon an evaluation of proposals submitted in response to a request for proposals prepared by or for a unit of local government.

(c)   The unit of local government shall require in its request for proposals that each proposal to be submitted shall include all of the following:

(1) Information relating to the experience of the proposer on the basis of which said proposer purports to be qualified to carry out all work required by a proposed contract; the ability of the proposer to secure adequate financing; and proposals for project staffing, implementation of work tasks, and the carrying out of all responsibilities required by a proposed contract.

(2) A proposal clearly identifying and specifying all elements of cost which would become charges to the unit of local government, in whatever form, in return for the fulfillment by the proposer of all tasks and responsibilities established by the request for the proposal for the full lifetime of a proposed contract, including, as appropriate, but not limited to, the cost of planning, design, construction, operation, management and/or maintenance of any facility; provided, that the unit of local government may prescribe the form and content of the proposal and that, in any event, the proposer must submit sufficiently detailed information to permit a fair and equitable evaluation of the proposal.

(3) Any other information as the unit of local government may determine to have a material bearing on its ability to evaluate any proposal in accordance with this section.

(d) Proposals received in response to a request for proposals may be evaluated on the basis of a technical analysis of facility design, operational experience of the technology to be utilized in the proposed facility, system reliability and availability, energy production balance and efficiency, environmental impact and protection, recovery of materials, required staffing level during operation, projection of anticipated revenues from the sale of energy and materials recovered by the facility, net cost to the unit of local government for operation and maintenance of the facility for the duration of time to be established in the request for proposals and upon any other factors and information that the unit of local government determined to have a material bearing on its ability to evaluate any proposal, which factors were set forth in said request for proposal.

(e) The unit of local government may make a contract award to any responsible proposer selected pursuant to this section based upon a determination that the selected proposal is more responsive to the request for proposals and may thereupon negotiate a contract with said proposer for the performance of the services set forth in the request for proposals and the response thereto, the determination shall be deemed to be conclusive. Notwithstanding other provisions of this Article or any local law, a contract may be negotiated and entered into between a unit of local government and any person selected as a responsible proposer hereunder which may provide for, but not be limited to, the following:

(1) A contract, lease, rental, license, permit or other authorization to design, construct, operate and maintain a solid waste or sludge management facility upon such terms and conditions, for such consideration, and for such duration, not to exceed 40 years, as may be agreed upon by the unit of local government and the person.

(2) Payment by the unit of local government of a fee or other charge to the person for acceptance, processing, recycling, management and disposal of solid waste or sludge.

(3) An obligation on the part of a unit of local government to deliver or cause to be delivered to a solid waste or sludge management facility guaranteed quantities of solid wastes or sludge.

(4) The sale, utilization or disposal of any form of energy, recovered material or residue resulting from the operation of any solid waste or sludge management facility.

(f) Except for authorities created pursuant to Article 22 of Chapter 153A of the General Statutes, the construction work for any facility or structure that is ancillary to a solid waste or sludge management facility and that does not involve storage and processing of solid waste or sludge or the separation, extraction, and recovery of useful or marketable forms of energy and materials from solid waste at a solid waste management facility shall be procured through competitive bidding procedures described by G.S. 143-128 through 143-129.1. Ancillary facilities include but are not limited to roads, water and sewer lines to the facility limits, transfer stations, scale houses, administration buildings, and residue and bypass disposal sites.

§ 143-129.4. Guaranteed energy savings contracts.

The solicitation and evaluation of proposals for guaranteed energy savings contracts, as defined in Part 2 of Article 3B of this Chapter, and the letting of contracts for these proposals are not governed by this Article but instead are governed by the provisions of that Part; except that guaranteed energy savings contracts are subject to the requirements of G.S. 143-128.2 and G.S. 143-135.3.

§ 143-132. Minimum number of bids for public contracts.

(a) No contract to which G.S. 143-129 applies for construction or repairs shall be awarded by any board or governing body of the State, or any subdivision thereof, unless at least three competitive bids have been received from reputable and qualified contractors regularly engaged in their respective lines of endeavor; however, this section shall not apply to contracts which are negotiated as provided for in G.S. 143-129. Provided that if after advertisement for bids as required by G.S. 143-129, not as many as three competitive bids have been received from reputable and qualified contractors regularly engaged in their respective lines of endeavor, said board or governing body of the State agency or of a county, city, town or other subdivision of the State shall again advertise for bids; and if as a result of such second advertisement, not as many as three competitive bids from reputable and qualified contractors are received, such board or governing body may then let the contract to the lowest responsible bidder submitting a bid for such project, even though only one bid is received.

(b) For purposes of contracts bid in the alternative between the separate-prime and single-prime contracts, pursuant to G.S. 143-128(d1) each single-prime bid shall constitute a competitive bid in each of the four subdivisions or branches of work listed in G.S. 143-128(a), and each full set of separate-prime bids shall constitute a competitive single-prime bid in meeting the requirements of subsection (a) of this section. If there are at least three single-prime bids but there is not at least one full set of separate-prime bids, no separate-prime bids shall be opened.

(c) The State Building Commission shall develop guidelines no later than January 1, 1991, governing the opening of bids pursuant to this Article. These guidelines shall be distributed to all public bodies subject to this Article. The guidelines shall not be subject to the provisions of Chapter 150B of the General Statutes.

§ 143-133.1. Reporting.

(a)　Governmental entities that contract with a construction manager at risk, design-builder, or private developer under a public-private partnership shall report to the Secretary of Administration the following information on all projects where a construction manager at risk, design-builder, or private developer under a public-private partnership is utilized:

(1)　A detailed explanation of the reason why the particular construction manager at risk, design-builder, or private developer was selected.

(2)　The terms of the contract with the construction manager at risk, design-builder, or private developer.

(3)　A list of all other firms considered but not selected as the construction manager at risk, design-builder, or private developer.

(4)　A report on the form of bidding utilized by the construction manager at risk, design-builder, or private developer on the project.

(5)　A detailed explanation of why the particular delivery method was used in lieu of the delivery methods identified in G.S. 143-128(a1) subdivisions (1) through (3) and the anticipated benefits to the public entity from using the particular delivery method.

(b)　The Secretary of Administration shall adopt rules to implement the provisions of this section, including the format and frequency of reporting.

(c)　A governmental entity letting a contract pursuant to any of the delivery methods identified in subdivisions (a1)(4), (a1)(6), (a1)(7), or (a1)(8) of G.S. 143-128 shall submit the report required by this section no later than 12 months from the date the governmental entity takes beneficial occupancy of the project. In the event that the governmental entity fails to do so, the governmental entity shall be prohibited from utilizing subdivisions (a1)(4), (a1)(6), (a1)(7), or (a1)(8) of G.S. 143-128 until such time as the governmental entity completes the reporting requirement under this this section. Contracts entered into in violation of this prohibition shall not be deemed ultra vires and shall remain valid and fully enforceable. Any person, corporation or entity, however, which has submitted a bid or response to a request for proposals on any construction project previously advertised by the governmental entity shall be entitled to obtain an injunction against the governmental entity compelling the governmental entity to comply with the reporting requirements of this section and from commencing or continuing a project let in violation of this subdivision until such time as the governmental entity has complied with the reporting requirements of this section. The plaintiff in such cases shall not be entitled to recover monetary damages caused by the governmental entity's failure to comply with this reporting requirements section, and neither the plaintiff nor the defendant shall be allowed to recover attorneys fees except as otherwise allowed by G.S. 1A-11 or G.S. 6-21.5. An action seeking the injunctive relief allowed by this subdivision must be filed within four years from the date that the owner governmental entity took beneficial occupancy of the project for which the report remains due.

(d)   For purposes of this section, the term "governmental entity" shall have the same meaning as in G.S. 143-128.1B(a)(6).

§ 143-134.1. Interest on final payments due to prime contractors; payments to subcontractors.

(a)   On all public construction contracts which are let by a board or governing body of the State government or any political subdivision thereof, except contracts let by the Department of Transportation pursuant to G.S. 136-28.1, the balance due prime contractors shall be paid in full within 45 days after respective prime contracts of the project have been accepted by the owner, certified by the architect, engineer or designer to be completed in accordance with terms of the plans and specifications, or occupied by the owner and used for the purpose for which the project was constructed, whichever occurs first. However, when the architect or consulting engineer in charge of the project determines that delay in completion of the project in accordance with terms of the plans and specifications is the fault of the contractor, the project may be occupied and used for the purposes for which it was constructed without payment of any interest on amounts withheld past the 45 day limit.

No payment shall be delayed because of the failure of another prime contractor on the project to complete his contract. Should final payment to any prime contractor beyond the date the contracts have been certified to be completed by the designer or architect, accepted by the owner, or occupied by the owner and used for the purposes for which the project was constructed, be delayed by more than 45 days, the prime contractor shall be paid interest, beginning on the 46th day, at the rate of one percent (1%) per month or fraction thereof unless a lower rate is agreed upon on the unpaid balance as may be due. In addition to the above final payment provisions, periodic payments due a prime contractor during construction shall be paid in accordance with the provisions of this section and the payment provisions of the contract documents that do not conflict with this section, or the prime contractor shall be paid interest on any unpaid amount at the rate stipulated above for delayed final payments. The interest shall begin on the date the payment is due and continue until the date on which payment is made. The due date may be established by the terms of the contract. Funds for payment of the interest on state-owned projects shall be obtained from the current budget of the owning department, institution, or agency. Where a conditional acceptance of a contract exists, and where the owner is retaining a reasonable sum pending correction of the conditions, interest on the reasonable sum shall not apply.

(b) Within seven days of receipt by the prime contractor of each periodic or final payment, the prime contractor shall pay the subcontractor based on work completed or service provided under the subcontract. If any periodic or final payment to the subcontractor is delayed by more than seven days after receipt of periodic or final payment by the prime contractor, the prime contractor shall pay the subcontractor interest, beginning on the eighth day, at the rate of one percent (1%) per month or fraction thereof on the unpaid balance as may be due.

(b1) No retainage on periodic or final payments made by the owner or prime contractor shall be allowed on public construction contracts in which the total project costs are less than one hundred thousand dollars ($100,000). Retainage on periodic or final payments on public construction contracts in which the total project costs are equal to or greater than one hundred thousand dollars ($100,000) is allowed as follows:

    (1) The owner shall not retain more than five percent (5%) of any periodic payment due a prime contractor.

    (2) When the project is fifty percent (50%) complete, the owner, with written consent of the surety, shall not retain any further retainage from periodic payments due the contractor if the contractor continues to perform satisfactorily and any nonconforming work identified in writing prior to that time by the architect, engineer, or owner has been corrected by the contractor and accepted by the architect, engineer, or owner. If the owner determines the contractor's performance is unsatisfactory, the owner may reinstate retainage for each

subsequent periodic payment application as authorized in this subsection up to the maximum amount of five percent (5%). The project shall be deemed fifty percent (50%) complete when the contractor's gross project invoices, excluding the value of materials stored off-site, equal or exceed fifty percent (50%) of the value of the contract, except the value of materials stored on-site shall not exceed twenty percent (20%) of the contractor's gross project invoices for the purpose of determining whether the project is fifty percent (50%) complete.

(3)   A subcontract on a contract governed by this section may include a provision for the retainage on periodic payments made by the prime contractor to the subcontractor. However, the percentage of the payment retained: (i) shall be paid to the subcontractor under the same terms and conditions as provided in subdivision (2) of this subsection and (ii) subject to subsection (b3) of this section, shall not exceed the percentage of retainage on payments made by the owner to the prime contractor. Subject to subsection (b3) of this section, any percentage of retainage on payments made by the prime contractor to the subcontractor that exceeds the percentage of retainage on payments made by the owner to the prime contractor shall be subject to interest to be paid by the prime contractor to the subcontractor at the rate of one percent (1%) per month or fraction thereof.

(4)   Within 60 days after the submission of a pay request and one of the following occurs, as specified in the contract documents, the owner with written consent of the surety shall release to the contractor all retainage on payments held by the owner: (i) the owner receives a certificate of substantial completion from the architect, engineer, or designer in charge of the project; or (ii) the owner receives beneficial occupancy or use of the project. However, the owner may retain sufficient funds to secure completion of the project or corrections on any work. If the owner retains funds, the amount retained shall not exceed two and one-half times the estimated value of the work to be completed or corrected.

> Any reduction in the amount of the retainage on payments shall be with the consent of the contractor's surety.
>
> (5) The existence of any third-party claims against the contractor or any additive change orders to the construction contract shall not be a basis for delaying the release of any retainage on payments.

(b2) Full payment, less authorized deductions, shall also be made for those trades that have reached one hundred percent (100%) completion of their contract by or before the project is fifty percent (50%) complete if the contractor has performed satisfactorily. However, payment to the early finishing trades is contingent upon the owner's receipt of an approval or certification from the architect of record or applicable engineer that the work performed by the subcontractor is acceptable and in accordance with the contract documents. At that time, the owner shall reduce the retainage for such trades to five-tenths percent (0.5%) of the contract. Payments under this subsection shall be made no later than 60 days following receipt of the subcontractor's request or immediately upon receipt of the surety's consent, whichever occurs later. Early finishing trades under this subsection shall include structural steel, piling, caisson, and demolition. The early finishing trades for which line-item release of retained funds is required shall not be construed to prevent an owner or an owner's representative from identifying any other trades not listed in this subsection that are also allowed line-item release of retained funds. Should the owner or owner's representative identify any other trades to be afforded line-item release of retainage, the trade shall be listed in the original bid documents. Each bid document shall list the inspections required by the owner before accepting the work, and any financial information required by the owner to release payment to the trades, except the failure of the bid documents to contain this information shall not obligate the owner to release the retainage if it has not received the required certification from the architect of record or applicable engineer.

(b3) Notwithstanding subdivisions (2) and (3) of subsection (b1) of this section, and subsection (b2) of this section, following fifty percent (50%) completion of the project, the owner shall be authorized to withhold additional retainage from a subsequent periodic payment, not to exceed five percent (5%) as set forth in subdivision (1) of subsection (b1) of this section, in order to allow the owner to retain two and one-half percent (2.5%)

total retainage through the completion of the project. In the event that the owner elects to withhold additional retainage on any periodic payment subsequent to release of retainage pursuant to subsection (b2) of this section, the general contractor may also withhold from the subcontractors remaining on the project sufficient retainage to offset the additional retainage held by the owner, notwithstanding the actual percentage of retainage withheld by the owner of the project as a whole.

(b4) Neither the owner's nor contractor's release of retainage on payments as part of a payment in full on a line-item of work under subsection (b2) of this section shall affect any applicable warranties on work done by the contractor or subcontractor, and the warranties shall not begin to run any earlier than either the owner's receipt of a certificate of substantial completion from the architect, engineer, or designer in charge of the project or the owner receives beneficial occupancy.

(b5) The State or any political subdivision of the State may allow contractors to bid on bonded projects with and without retainage on payments.

(b6) Nothing in subsections (b1), (b2), (b3), and (b4) of this section shall operate to prevent any agency or any political subdivision of the State from complying with the requirements of a federal contract or grant when the requirements of the federal contract or grant conflict with subsections (b1), (b2), (b3), or (b4) of this section. Each bid document must specify when federal preemption of this section shall apply.

(c) Repealed by Session Laws 2007-365, s. 1, effective January 1, 2008.

(d) Nothing in this section shall prevent the prime contractor at the time of application and certification to the owner from withholding application and certification to the owner for payment to the subcontractor for unsatisfactory job progress; defective construction not remedied; disputed work; third[-]party claims filed or reasonable evidence that claim will be filed; failure of subcontractor to make timely payments for labor, equipment, and materials; damage to prime contractor or another subcontractor; reasonable evidence that subcontract cannot be completed for the unpaid balance of the subcontract sum; or a reasonable amount for retainage not to exceed the initial percentage retained by the owner.

(e) Nothing in this section shall prevent the owner from withholding payment to the contractor in addition to the amounts authorized by this section for unsatisfactory job progress, defective construction not reme-

died, disputed work, or third-party claims filed against the owner or reasonable evidence that a third-party claim will be filed.

§ 143-134.2. Actions by contractor on behalf of subcontractor.

(a)   A contractor may, on behalf of a subcontractor of any tier under
the contractor, file an action against an owner regarding a claim arising out
of or relating to labor, materials, or services furnished by the subcontractor
to the contractor pursuant to a contract between the subcontractor and the
contractor for the same project that is the subject of the contract between
the contractor and the owner.

(b)   In any action filed by a contractor against an owner under subsection (a) of this section, it shall not be a defense that the costs and damages
at issue were incurred by a subcontractor and that subcontractor has not
been paid for these costs and damages. The owner shall not be required to
pay the contractor for the costs and damages incurred by a subcontractor,
unless the subcontractor submits proof to the court that the contractor has
paid these costs and damages to the subcontractor.

§ 143-135. Limitation of application of Article.

Except for the provisions of G.S. 143-129 requiring bids for the purchase
of apparatus, supplies, materials or equipment, this Article shall not apply
to construction or repair work undertaken by the State or by subdivisions
of the State of North Carolina (i) when the work is performed by duly
elected officers or agents using force account qualified labor on the permanent payroll of the agency concerned and (ii) when either the total cost
of the project, including without limitation all direct and indirect costs
of labor, services, materials, supplies and equipment, does not exceed one
hundred twenty-five thousand dollars ($125,000) or the total cost of labor
on the project does not exceed fifty thousand dollars ($50,000); provided
that, for The University of North Carolina and its constituent institutions,
force account qualified labor may be used (i) when the work is performed
by duly elected officers or agents using force account qualified labor on the
permanent payroll of the university and (ii) when either the total cost of the
project, including, without limitation, all direct and indirect costs of labor,
services, materials, supplies, and equipment, does not exceed two hundred
thousand dollars ($200,000) or the total cost of labor on the project does
not exceed one hundred thousand dollars ($100,000). This force account

work shall be subject to the approval of the Director of the Budget in the case of State agencies, of the responsible commission, council, or board in the case of subdivisions of the State. Complete and accurate records of the entire cost of such work, including without limitation, all direct and indirect costs of labor, services, materials, supplies and equipment performed and furnished in the prosecution and completion thereof, shall be maintained by such agency, commission, council or board for the inspection by the general public. Construction or repair work undertaken pursuant to this section shall not be divided for the purposes of evading the provisions of this Article.

§ 143-135.5. State policy; cooperation in promoting the use of small, minority, physically handicapped and women contractors; purpose.

(a)   It is the policy of this State to encourage and promote the use of small, minority, physically handicapped and women contractors in State construction projects. All State agencies, institutions and political subdivisions shall cooperate with the Department of Administration and all other State agencies, institutions and political subdivisions in efforts to encourage and promote the use of small, minority, physically handicapped and women contractors in achieving the purpose of this Article, which is the effective and economical construction of public buildings.

(b)   It is the policy of this State not to accept bids or proposals from, nor to engage in business with, any business that, within the last two years, has been finally found by a court or an administrative agency of competent jurisdiction to have unlawfully discriminated on the basis of race, gender, religion, national origin, age, physical disability, or any other unlawful basis in its solicitation, selection, hiring, or treatment of another business.

§ 143-135.8. Prequalification.

(a)   Except as provided in this section, bidders may not be prequalified for any construction or repair work project.

(b)   A governmental entity may prequalify bidders for a particular construction or repair work project when all of the following apply:

    (1)   The governmental entity is using one of the construction methods authorized in G.S. 143-128(a1)(1) through G.S. 143-128(a1)(3).

(2) The board or governing body of the governmental entity adopts an objective prequalification policy applicable to all construction or repair work prior to the advertisement of the contract for which the governmental entity intends to prequalify bidders.

(3) The governmental entity has adopted the assessment tool and criteria for that specific project, which must include the prequalification scoring values and minimum required score for prequalification on that project.

(c) The objective prequalification policy adopted by a governmental entity pursuant to subdivision (2) of subsection (b) of this section shall meet all of the following criteria:

(1) Must be uniform, consistent, and transparent in its application to all bidders.

(2) Must allow all bidders who meet the prequalification criteria to be prequalified to bid on the construction or repair work project.

(3) Clearly state the prequalification criteria, which must comply with all of the following:

a. Be rationally related to construction or repair work.

b. Not require that the bidder has previously been awarded a construction or repair project by the governmental entity.

c. Permit bidders to submit history or experience with projects of similar size, scope, or complexity.

(4) Clearly state the assessment process of the criteria to be used.

(5) Establish a process for a denied bidder to protest to the governmental entity denial of prequalification, which process shall be completed prior to the opening of bids under G.S. 143-129(b) and which allows sufficient time for a bidder subsequently prequalified pursuant to a protest to submit a bid on the contract for which the bidder is subsequently prequalified.

(6) Outline a process by which the basis for denial of prequalification will be communicated in writing, upon request, to a bidder who is denied prequalification.

(d) If the governmental entity opts to prequalify bidders, bids submitted by any bidder not prequalified shall be deemed nonresponsive. This subsection shall not apply to bidders initially denied prequalification that are subsequently prequalified pursuant to a protest under the governmental entity's prequalification policy.

(e) Prequalification may not be used for the selection of any qualification-based services under Article 3D of this Chapter, G.S. 143-128.1A, G.S. 143-128.1B, G.S. 143-128.1C, or the selection of the construction manager at risk under G.S. 143-128.1.

(f) For purposes of this section, the following definitions shall apply:

    (1) Governmental entity. – As defined in G.S. 143-128.1B(a)(6).

    (2) Prequalification. – A process of evaluating and determining whether potential bidders have the skill, judgment, integrity, sufficient financial resources, and ability necessary to the faithful performance of a contract for construction or repair work.

§ 44A-26. Bonds required.

(a) When the total amount of construction contracts awarded for any one project exceeds three hundred thousand dollars ($300,000), a performance and payment bond as set forth in (1) and (2) is required by the contracting body from any contractor or construction manager at risk with a contract more than fifty thousand dollars ($50,000); provided that, for State departments, State agencies, and The University of North Carolina and its constituent institutions, a performance and payment bond is required in accordance with this subsection if the total amount of construction contracts awarded for any one project exceeds five hundred thousand dollars ($500,000). In the discretion of the contracting body, a performance and payment bond may be required on any construction contract as follows:

    (1) A performance bond in the amount of one hundred percent (100%) of the construction contract amount, conditioned upon the faithful performance of the contract in accordance with the plans, specifications and conditions of the contract. Such bond shall be solely for the protection of the contracting body that is constructing the project.

    (2) A payment bond in the amount of one hundred percent (100%) of the construction contract amount, conditioned

upon the prompt payment for all labor or materials for which a contractor or subcontractor is liable. The payment bond shall be solely for the protection of the persons furnishing materials or performing labor for which a contractor, subcontractor, or construction manager at risk is liable.

(b) The performance bond and the payment bond shall be executed by one or more surety companies legally authorized to do business in the State of North Carolina and shall become effective upon the awarding of the construction contract.

§ 87-1. "General contractor" defined; exceptions.

(a) For the purpose of this Article any person or firm or corporation who for a fixed price, commission, fee, or wage, undertakes to bid upon or to construct or who undertakes to superintend or manage, on his own behalf or for any person, firm, or corporation that is not licensed as a general contractor pursuant to this Article, the construction of any building, highway, public utilities, grading or any improvement or structure where the cost of the undertaking is thirty thousand dollars ($30,000) or more, or undertakes to erect a North Carolina labeled manufactured modular building meeting the North Carolina State Building Code, shall be deemed to be a "general contractor" engaged in the business of general contracting in the State of North Carolina.

(b) This section shall not apply to the following:

(1) Persons, firms, or corporations furnishing or erecting industrial equipment, power plan equipment, radial brick chimneys, and monuments.

(2) Any person, firm, or corporation who constructs or alters a building on land owned by that person, firm, or corporation provided (i) the building is intended solely for occupancy by that person and his family, firm, or corporation after completion; and (ii) the person, firm, or corporation complies with G.S. 87-14. If the building is not occupied solely by the person and his family, firm, or corporation for at least 12 months following completion, it shall be presumed that the person, firm, or corporation did not intend the building solely for occupancy by that person and his family, firm, or corporation.

(3) Any person engaged in the business of farming who constructs or alters a building on land owned by that person and used in the business of farming, when the building is intended for use by that person after completion.

§ 87-14. Regulations as to issue of building permits.

(a) Any person, firm, or corporation, upon making application to the building inspector or such other authority of any incorporated city, town, or county in North Carolina charged with the duty of issuing building or other permits for the construction of any building, highway, sewer, grading, or any improvement or structure where the cost thereof is to be thirty thousand dollars ($30,000) or more, shall, before being entitled to the issuance of a permit, satisfy the following:

(1) Furnish satisfactory proof to the inspector or authority that the person seeking the permit or another person contracting to superintend or manage the construction is duly licensed under the terms of this Article to carry out or superintend the construction or is exempt from licensure under G.S. 87-1(b). If an applicant claims an exemption from licensure pursuant to G.S. 87-1(b)(2), the applicant for the building permit shall execute a verified affidavit attesting to the following:

a. That the person is the owner of the property on which the building is being constructed or, in the case of a firm or corporation, is legally authorized to act on behalf of the firm or corporation.

b. That the person will personally superintend and manage all aspects of the construction of the building and that the duty will not be delegated to any other person not duly licensed under the terms of this Article.

c. That the person will be personally present for all inspections required by the North Carolina State Building Code, unless the plans for the building were drawn and sealed by an architect licensed pursuant to Chapter 83A of the General Statutes.

The building inspector or other authority shall transmit a copy of the affidavit to the Board, who shall verify that the applicant was validly entitled to claim the exemption under

G.S. 87-1(b)(2). If the Board determines that the applicant was not entitled to claim the exemption under G.S. 87-1(b)(2), the building permit shall be revoked pursuant to G.S. 153A-362 or G.S. 160A-422.

(2) Furnish proof that the person has in effect Workers' Compensation insurance as required by Chapter 97 of the General Statutes.

(3) Any person, firm, or corporation, upon making application to the building inspector or such other authority of any incorporated city, town, or county in North Carolina charged with the duty of issuing building permits pursuant to G.S. 160A-417(a)(1) or G.S. 153A-357(a)(1) for any improvements for which the combined cost is to be thirty thousand dollars ($30,000) or more, other than for improvements to an existing single-family residential dwelling unit as defined in G.S. 87-15.5(7) that the owner occupies as a residence, or for the addition of an accessory building or accessory structure as defined in the North Carolina Uniform Residential Building Code, the use of which is incidental to that residential dwelling unit, shall be required to provide to the building inspector or other authority the name, physical and mailing address, telephone number, facsimile number, and electronic mail address of the lien agent designated by the owner pursuant to G.S. 44A-11.1(a).

(b) It shall be unlawful for the building inspector or other authority to issue or allow the issuance of a building permit pursuant to this section unless and until the applicant has furnished evidence that the applicant is either exempt from the provisions of this Article and, if applicable, fully complied with the provisions of subdivision (a)(1) of this section, or is duly licensed under this Article to carry out or superintend the work for which permit has been applied; and further, that the applicant has in effect Workers' Compensation insurance as required by Chapter 97 of the General Statutes. Any building inspector or other authority who is subject to and violates the terms of this section shall be guilty of a Class 3 misdemeanor and subject only to a fine of not more than fifty dollars ($50.00).

§ 87-15. Copy of Article included in specifications; bid not considered unless contractor licensed.

All architects and engineers preparing plans and specifications for work to be contracted in the State of North Carolina shall include in their invitations to bidders and in their specifications a copy of this Article or such portions thereof as are deemed necessary to convey to the invited bidder, whether he be a resident or nonresident of this State and whether a license has been issued to him or not, the information that it will be necessary for him to show evidence of a license before his bid is considered.

§ 133-1.1. Certain buildings involving public funds to be designed, etc., by architect or engineer.

(a)   In the interest of public health, safety and economy, every officer, board, department, or commission charged with the duty of approving plans and specifications or awarding or entering into contracts involving the expenditure of public funds in excess of:

   (1)   Three hundred thousand dollars ($300,000) for the repair of public buildings where such repair does not include major structural change in framing or foundation support systems, or five hundred thousand dollars ($500,000) for the repair of public buildings by The University of North Carolina or its constituent institutions where such repair does not include major structural change in framing or foundation support systems,

   (1a)   One hundred thousand dollars ($100,000) for the repair of public buildings affecting life safety systems,

   (2)   One hundred thirty-five thousand dollars ($135,000) for the repair of public buildings where such repair includes major structural change in framing or foundation support systems, or

   (3)   One hundred thirty-five thousand dollars ($135,000) for the construction of, or additions to, public buildings or State-owned and operated utilities, shall require that such plans and specifications be prepared by a registered architect, in accordance with the provisions of Chapter 83A of the General Statutes, or by a registered engineer, in accordance with the provisions of Chapter 89C of the General Statutes, or by

both architect and engineer, particularly qualified by training and experience for the type of work involved, and that the North Carolina seal of such architect or engineer together with the name and address of such architect or engineer, or both, be placed on all these plans and specifications.

(b) (1) On all projects requiring the services of an architect, an architect shall conduct frequent and regular inspections or such inspections as required by contract and shall issue a signed and sealed certificate of compliance to the awarding authority that:

    a. The inspections of the construction, repairs or installations have been conducted with the degree of care and professional skill and judgment ordinarily exercised by a member of that profession; and

    b. To the best of his knowledge and in the professional opinion of the architect, the contractor has fulfilled the obligations of such plans, specifications, and contract.

(2) On all projects requiring the services of an engineer, an engineer shall conduct frequent and regular inspections or such inspections as required by contract and shall issue a signed and sealed certificate of compliance to the awarding authority that:

    a. The inspections of the construction, repairs, or installations have been conducted with the degree of care and professional skill and judgment ordinarily exercised by a member of that profession; and

    b. To the best of his knowledge and in the professional opinion of the engineer, the contractor has fulfilled the obligations of such plans, specifications, and contract.

(3) No certificate of compliance shall be issued until the architect and/or engineer is satisfied that the contractor has fulfilled the obligations of such plans, specifications, and contract.

(c) The following shall be excepted from the requirements of subsection (a) of this section:

(1) Dwellings and outbuildings in connection therewith, such as barns and private garages.

(2) Apartment buildings used exclusively as the residence of not more than two families.

(3) Buildings used for agricultural purposes other than schools or assembly halls which are not within the limits of a city or an incorporated village.

(4) Temporary buildings or sheds used exclusively for construction purposes, not exceeding 20 feet in any direction, and not used for living quarters.

(5) Pre-engineered garages, sheds, and workshops up to 5,000 square feet used exclusively by city, county, public school, or State employees for purposes related to their employment. For pre-engineered garages, sheds, and workshops constructed pursuant to this subdivision, there shall be a minimum separation of these structures from other buildings or property lines of 30 feet.

(d) On projects on which no registered architect or engineer is required pursuant to the provisions of this section, the governing board or awarding authority shall require a certificate of compliance with the State Building Code from the city or county inspector for the specific trade or trades involved or from a registered architect or engineer, except that the provisions of this subsection shall not apply to projects where any of the following apply:

(1) The plans and specifications are approved by the Department of Administration, Division of State Construction, and the completed project is inspected by the Division of State Construction and the State Electrical Inspector.

(2) The project is exempt from the State Building Code.

(3) The project has a total projected cost of less than $100,000 and does not alter life safety systems.

(e) All plans and specifications for public buildings of any kind shall be identified by the name and address of the author thereof.

(f) Neither the designer nor the contractor involved shall receive his final payment until the required certificate of compliance shall have been received by the awarding authority.

(g) On all facilities which are covered by this Article, other than those listed in subsection (c) of this section and which require any job-installed finishes, the plans and specifications shall include the color schedule.

§ 133-3. Specifications to carry competitive items; substitution of materials.

All architects, engineers, designers, or draftsmen, when providing design services, or writing specifications, directly or indirectly, for materials to be used in any city, county or State work, shall specify in their plans the required performance and design characteristics of such materials. However, when it is impossible or impractical to specify the required performance and design characteristics for such materials, then the architect, engineer, designer or draftsman may use a brand name specification so long as they cite three or more examples of items of equal design or equivalent design, which would establish an acceptable range for items of equal or equivalent design. The specifications shall state clearly that the cited examples are used only to denote the quality standard of product desired and that they do not restrict bidders to a specific brand, make, manufacturer or specific name; that they are used only to set forth and convey to bidders the general style, type, character and quality of product desired; and that equivalent products will be acceptable. Where it is impossible to specify performance and design characteristics for such materials and impossible to cite three or more items due to the fact that there are not that many items of similar or equivalent design in competition, then as many items as are available shall be cited. On all city, county or State works, the maximum interchangeability and compatibility of cited items shall be required. The brand of product used on a city, county or State work shall not limit competitive bidding on future works. Specifications may list one or more preferred brands as an alternate to the base bid in limited circumstances. Specifications containing a preferred brand alternate under this section must identify the performance standards that support the preference. Performance standards for the preference must be approved in advance by the owner in an open meeting. Any alternate approved by the owner shall be approved only where (i) the preferred alternate will provide cost savings, maintain or improve the functioning of any process or system affected by the preferred item or items, or both, and (ii) a justification identifying these criteria is made available in writing to the public. Substitution of materials, items, or equipment of equal or equivalent design shall be submitted to the architect or engineer for approval or disapproval; such approval or disapproval shall be made by the architect or engineer prior to the opening of bids. The purpose of this statute is to mandate and encourage free and open competition on public contracts.

§ 133-4. Violation of Chapter made misdemeanor.

Any person, firm, or corporation violating the provisions of this Chapter shall be guilty of a Class 3 misdemeanor and upon conviction, license to practice his profession in this State shall be withdrawn for a period of one year and he shall only be subject to a fine of not more than five hundred dollars ($500.00).

§ 58-31-40. Commissioner to inspect State property.

(a)   The Commissioner shall, as often as is required in the fire code adopted by the North Carolina Building Code Council or more often if the Commissioner considers it necessary, visit, inspect, and thoroughly examine every State property to analyze and determine its protection from fire, including the property's occupants or contents. The Commissioner shall notify in writing the agency or official in charge of the property of any defect noted by the Commissioner or any improvement considered by the Commissioner to be necessary, and a copy of that notice shall be forwarded by the Commissioner to the Department of Administration.

(b)   No agency or person authorized or directed by law to select a plan or erect a building comprising 20,000 square feet or more for the use of any county, city, or school district shall receive and approve of the plan until it is submitted to and approved by the Commissioner as to the safety of the proposed building from fire, including the property's occupants or contents.

(c)   Repealed by Session Laws 2009-474, s. 1, effective October 1, 2009.

C. Qualifications-Based Selection

§ 143-64.31. Declaration of public policy.

(a)   It is the public policy of this State and all public subdivisions and Local Governmental Units thereof, except in cases of special emergency involving the health and safety of the people or their property, to announce all requirements for architectural, engineering, surveying, construction management at risk services, design-build services, and public-private partnership construction services to select firms qualified to provide such services on the basis of demonstrated competence and qualification for the type of professional services required without regard to fee other than unit price information at this stage, and thereafter to negotiate a contract for those services at a fair and reasonable fee with the best qualified firm. If a contract cannot be negotiated with the best qualified firm, negotiations with that firm shall be terminated and initiated with the next best qualified firm. Selection of a firm under this Article shall include the use of good faith efforts by the public entity to notify minority firms of the opportunity to submit qualifications for consideration by the public entity.

(a1)   A resident firm providing architectural, engineering, surveying, construction management at risk services, design-build services, or public-private partnership construction services shall be granted a preference over a nonresident firm, in the same manner, on the same basis, and to the extent that a preference is granted in awarding contracts for these services by the other state to its resident firms over firms resident in the State of North Carolina. For purposes of this section, a resident firm is a firm that has paid unemployment taxes or income taxes in North Carolina and whose principal place of business is located in this State.

[*Note: S.L. 2014-42, sec. 3, recodified G.S. 143-64.31(b)–(d) as G.S. 143-133.1(a)–(c). (See page 108 for the latest version of G.S. 143-133.1.)*]

(e)   For purposes of this Article, the definition in G.S. 143-128.1B and G.S. 143-128.1C shall apply.

(f)   Except as provided in this subsection, no work product or design may be solicited, submitted, or considered as part of the selection process under this Article; and no costs or fees, other than unit price information, may be solicited, submitted, or considered as part of the selection process under this Article. Examples of prior completed work may be solicited, submitted, and considered when determining demonstrated competence and qualification of professional services; and discussion of concepts or approaches to the project, including impact on project schedules, is encouraged.

§ 143-64.32. Written exemption of particular contracts.

Units of local government or the North Carolina Department of Transportation may in writing exempt particular projects from the provisions of this Article in the case of proposed projects where an estimated professional fee is in an amount less than fifty thousand dollars ($50,000).

§ 143-64.33. Advice in selecting consultants or negotiating consultant contracts.

On architectural, engineering, or surveying contracts, the Department of Transportation or the Department of Administration may provide, upon request by a county, city, town or other subdivision of the State, advice in the process of selecting consultants or in negotiating consultant contracts with architects, engineers, or surveyors or any or all.

§ 143-64.34. Exemption of certain projects.

State capital improvement projects under the jurisdiction of the State Building Commission, capital improvement projects of The University of North Carolina, and community college capital improvement projects, where the estimated expenditure of public money is less than five hundred thousand dollars ($500,000), are exempt from the provisions of this Article.

D. Conflicts of Interest and Other Limitations

§ 14-234. Public officers or employees benefiting from public contracts; exceptions.

(a) (1) No public officer or employee who is involved in making or administering a contract on behalf of a public agency may derive a direct benefit from the contract except as provided in this section, or as otherwise allowed by law.

      (2) A public officer or employee who will derive a direct benefit from a contract with the public agency he or she serves, but who is not involved in making or administering the contract, shall not attempt to influence any other person who is involved in making or administering the contract.

      (3) No public officer or employee may solicit or receive any gift, favor, reward, service, or promise of reward, including a

promise of future employment, in exchange for recommending, influencing, or attempting to influence the award of a contract by the public agency he or she serves.

(a1) For purposes of this section:

(1) As used in this section, the term "public officer" means an individual who is elected or appointed to serve or represent a public agency, other than an employee or independent contractor of a public agency.

(2) A public officer or employee is involved in administering a contract if he or she oversees the performance of the contract or has authority to make decisions regarding the contract or to interpret the contract.

(3) A public officer or employee is involved in making a contract if he or she participates in the development of specifications or terms or in the preparation or award of the contract. A public officer is also involved in making a contract if the board, commission, or other body of which he or she is a member takes action on the contract, whether or not the public officer actually participates in that action, unless the contract is approved under an exception to this section under which the public officer is allowed to benefit and is prohibited from voting.

(4) A public officer or employee derives a direct benefit from a contract if the person or his or her spouse: (i) has more than a ten percent (10%) ownership or other interest in an entity that is a party to the contract; (ii) derives any income or commission directly from the contract; or (iii) acquires property under the contract.

(5) A public officer or employee is not involved in making or administering a contract solely because of the performance of ministerial duties related to the contract.

(b) Subdivision (a)(1) of this section does not apply to any of the following:

(1) Any contract between a public agency and a bank, banking institution, savings and loan association, or with a public utility regulated under the provisions of Chapter 62 of the General Statutes.

(2) An interest in property conveyed by an officer or employee of a public agency under a judgment, including a consent judgment, entered by a superior court judge in a condemnation proceeding initiated by the public agency.

(3) Any employment relationship between a public agency and the spouse of a public officer of the agency.

(4) Remuneration from a public agency for services, facilities, or supplies furnished directly to needy individuals by a public officer or employee of the agency under any program of direct public assistance being rendered under the laws of this State or the United States to needy persons administered in whole or in part by the agency if: (i) the programs of public assistance to needy persons are open to general participation on a nondiscriminatory basis to the practitioners of any given profession, professions or occupation; (ii) neither the agency nor any of its employees or agents, have control over who, among licensed or qualified providers, shall be selected by the beneficiaries of the assistance; (iii) the remuneration for the services, facilities or supplies are in the same amount as would be paid to any other provider; and (iv) although the public officer or employee may participate in making determinations of eligibility of needy persons to receive the assistance, he or she takes no part in approving his or her own bill or claim for remuneration.

(b1) No public officer who will derive a direct benefit from a contract entered into under subsection (b) of this section may deliberate or vote on the contract or attempt to influence any other person who is involved in making or administering the contract.

(c) through (d) Repealed by Session Laws 2001-409, s. 1, effective July 1, 2002.

(d1) Subdivision (a)(1) of this section does not apply to (i) any elected official or person appointed to fill an elective office of a village, town, or city having a population of no more than 15,000 according to the most recent official federal census, (ii) any elected official or person appointed to fill an elective office of a county within which there is located no village, town, or city with a population of more than 15,000 according to the most recent official federal census, (iii) any elected official or person appointed to fill an elective office on a city board of education in a city having a population of no more than 15,000 according to the most recent official federal census, (iv) any elected official or person appointed to fill an elective office as a member of a county board of education in a county within which there is located no village, town or city with a population of more than 15,000 according to the most recent official federal census, (v) any physician, pharmacist, dentist, optometrist, veterinarian, or nurse appointed to a county social services board, local health board, or area mental health, developmental disabilities, and substance abuse board serving one or more counties within which there is located no village, town, or city with a population of more than 15,000 according to the most recent official federal census, and (vi) any member of the board of directors of a public hospital if all of the following apply:

(1) The undertaking or contract or series of undertakings or contracts between the village, town, city, county, county social services board, county or city board of education, local health board or area mental health, developmental disabilities, and substance abuse board, or public hospital and one of its officials is approved by specific resolution of the governing body adopted in an open and public meeting, and recorded in its minutes and the amount does not exceed twenty thousand dollars ($20,000) for medically related services and forty thousand dollars ($40,000) for other goods or services within a 12-month period.

(2) The official entering into the contract with the unit or agency does not participate in any way or vote.

(3) The total annual amount of contracts with each official, shall be specifically noted in the audited annual financial statement of the village, town, city, or county.

(4) The governing board of any village, town, city, county, county social services board, county or city board of education, local health board, area mental health, developmental disabilities, and substance abuse board, or public hospital which contracts with any of the officials of their governmental unit shall post in a conspicuous place in its village, town, or city hall, or courthouse, as the case may be, a list of all such officials with whom such contracts have been made, briefly

describing the subject matter of the undertakings or contracts and showing their total amounts; this list shall cover the preceding 12 months and shall be brought uptodate at least quarterly.

(d2) Subsection (d1) of this section does not apply to contracts that are subject to Article 8 of Chapter 143 of the General Statutes, Public Building Contracts.

(d3) Subsection (a) of this section does not apply to an application for or the receipt of a grant under the Agriculture Cost Share Program for Nonpoint Source Pollution Control created pursuant to Article 72 of Chapter 106 of the General Statutes, the Community Conservation Assistance Program created pursuant to Article 73 of Chapter 106 of the General Statutes, or the Agricultural Water Resources Assistance Program created pursuant to Article 5 of Chapter 139 of the General Statutes by a member of the Soil and Water Conservation Commission if the requirements of G.S. 139-4(e) are met, and does not apply to a district supervisor of a soil and water conservation district if the requirements of G.S. 139-8(b) are met.

(d4) Subsection (a) of this section does not apply to an application for, or the receipt of a grant or other financial assistance from, the Tobacco Trust Fund created under Article 75 of Chapter 143 of the General Statutes by a member of the Tobacco Trust Fund Commission or an entity in which a member of the Commission has an interest provided that the requirements of G.S. 143-717(h) are met.

(d5) This section does not apply to a public hospital subject to G.S. 131E-14.2 or a public hospital authority subject to G.S. 131E-21.

(d6) This section does not apply to employment contracts between the State Board of Education and its chief executive officer.

(e) Anyone violating this section shall be guilty of a Class 1 misdemeanor.

(f) A contract entered into in violation of this section is void. A contract that is void under this section may continue in effect until an alternative can be arranged when: (i) immediate termination would result in harm to the public health or welfare, and (ii) the continuation is approved as provided in this subsection. A public agency that is a party to the contract may request approval to continue contracts under this subsection as follows:

    (1) Local governments, as defined in G.S. 159-7(15), public authorities, as defined in G.S. 159-7(10), local school administrative

units, and community colleges may request approval from the chair of the Local Government Commission.

(2) All other public agencies may request approval from the State Director of the Budget.

Approval of continuation of contracts under this subsection shall be given for the minimum period necessary to protect the public health or welfare.

§ 133-32. Gifts and favors regulated.

(a) It shall be unlawful for any contractor, subcontractor, or supplier who:

(1) Has a contract with a governmental agency; or

(2) Has performed under such a contract within the past year; or

(3) Anticipates bidding on such a contract in the future

to make gifts or to give favors to any officer or employee of a governmental agency who is charged with the duty of:

(1) Preparing plans, specifications, or estimates for public contract; or

(2) Awarding or administering public contracts; or

(3) Inspecting or supervising construction.

It shall also be unlawful for any officer or employee of a governmental agency who is charged with the duty of:

(1) Preparing plans, specifications, or estimates for public contracts; or

(2) Awarding or administering public contracts; or

(3) Inspecting or supervising construction willfully to receive or accept any such gift or favor.

(b) A violation of subsection (a) shall be a Class 1 misdemeanor.

(c) Gifts or favors made unlawful by this section shall not be allowed as a deduction for North Carolina tax purposes by any contractor, subcontractor or supplier or officers or employees thereof.

(d) This section is not intended to prevent a gift a public servant would be permitted to accept under G.S. 138A-32, or the gift and receipt of honorariums for participating in meetings, advertising items or souvenirs of nominal value, or meals furnished at banquets. This section is not intended to prevent any contractor, subcontractor, or supplier from making donations to professional organizations to defray meeting expenses where governmental employees are members of such professional organizations, nor is it intended to prevent governmental employees who are members of professional organizations from participation in all scheduled meeting functions available to all members of the professional organization attending the meeting. This section is also not intended to prohibit customary gifts or favors between employees or officers and their friends and relatives or the friends and relatives of their spouses, minor children, or members of their household where it is clear that it is that relationship rather than the business of the individual concerned which is the motivating factor for the gift or favor. However, all such gifts knowingly made or received are required to be reported by the donee to the agency head if the gifts are made by a contractor, subcontractor, or supplier doing business directly or indirectly with the governmental agency employing the recipient of such a gift.

§ 133-24. Government contracts; violation of G.S. 75-1 and 75-2.

Every person who shall engage in any conspiracy, combination, or any other act in restraint of trade or commerce declared to be unlawful by the provisions of G.S. 75-1 and 75-2 shall be guilty of a felony under this section where the combination, conspiracy, or other unlawful act in restraint of trade involves:

(1) A contract for the purchase of equipment, goods, services or materials or for construction or repair let or to be let by a governmental agency;

(2) A subcontract for the purchase of equipment, goods, services or materials or for construction or repair with a prime contractor or proposed prime contractor for a governmental agency.

§ 133-25. Conviction; punishment.

(a) Upon conviction of violating G.S. 133-24, any person shall be punished as a Class H felon. The court may also impose a fine of up to one hundred thousand dollars ($100,000) on any convicted individual and a fine of up to one million dollars ($1,000,000) on any convicted corporation.

Any fine imposed pursuant to this section shall not be deductible on a State income tax return for any purpose.

(b)   For a period of up to three years from the date of conviction, said period to be determined in the discretion of the court, no person shall be eligible to enter into a contract with any governmental agency, either directly as a contractor or indirectly as a subcontractor, if that person has been convicted of violating G.S. 133-24.

(c)   In the event an individual is convicted of violating G.S. 133-24, the court may, in its discretion, for a period of up to three years from the date of conviction, provide that the individual shall not be employed by a corporation as an officer, director, employee or agent, if that corporation engages in public construction or repair contracts with a governmental agency, either directly as a contractor or indirectly as a subcontractor.

(d)   The court shall also have authority to direct the appropriate contractor's licensing board to suspend the license of any contractor convicted of violating G.S. 133-24 for a period of up to three years from the date of conviction.

§ 133-27. Suspension from bidding.

Any governmental agency shall have the authority to suspend for a period of up to three years from the date of conviction any person and any subsidiary or affiliate of any person from further bidding to the agency and from being a subcontractor to a contractor for the agency and from being a supplier to the agency if that person or any officer, director, employee or agent of that person has been convicted of charges of engaging in any conspiracy, combination, or other unlawful act in restraint of trade or of similar charges in any federal court or a court of any other state.

A governmental agency may order a temporary suspension of any contractor, subcontractor, or supplier or subsidiary or affiliate thereof charged in an indictment or an information with engaging in any conspiracy, combination, or other unlawful act in restraint of trade or of similar charges in any federal court or a court of this or any other state until the charges are resolved.

The provisions of this section are in addition to and not in derogation of any other powers and authority of any governmental agency.

§ 133-30. Noncollusion affidavits.

Noncollusion affidavits may be required by rule of any governmental agency from all prime bidders. Any such requirement shall be set forth in the invitation to bid. Failure of any bidder to provide a required affidavit to the governmental agency shall be grounds for disqualification of his bid. The provisions of this section are in addition to and not in derogation of any other powers and authority of any governmental agency.

§ 133-33. Cost estimates; bidders' lists.

Any governmental agency responsible for letting public contracts may promulgate rules concerning the confidentiality of:

 (1) The agency's cost estimate for any public contracts prior to bidding; and

 (2) The identity of contractors who have obtained proposals for bid purposes for a public contract.

If the agency's rules require that such information be kept confidential, an employee or officer of the agency who divulges such information to any unauthorized person shall be subject to disciplinary action. This section shall not be construed to require that cost estimates or bidders' lists be kept confidential.

§ 14-234.1. Misuse of confidential information.

 (a) It is unlawful for any officer or employee of the State or an officer or an employee of any of its political subdivisions, in contemplation of official action by himself or by a governmental unit with which he is associated, or in reliance on information which was made known to him in his official capacity and which has not been made public, to commit any of the following acts:

 (1) Acquire a pecuniary interest in any property, transaction, or enterprise or gain any pecuniary benefit which may be affected by such information or official action; or

 (2) Intentionally aid another to do any of the above acts.

 (b) Violation of this section is a Class 1 misdemeanor.

§ 143-58.1. Unauthorized use of public purchase or contract procedures for private benefit.

(a)   It shall be unlawful for any person, by the use of the powers, policies or procedures described in this Article or established hereunder, to purchase, attempt to purchase, procure or attempt to procure any property or services for private use or benefit.

(b)   This prohibition shall not apply if:

(1)   The department, institution or agency through which the property or services are procured had theretofore established policies and procedures permitting such purchases or procurement by a class or classes of persons in order to provide for the mutual benefit of such persons and the department, institution or agency involved, or the public benefit or convenience; and

(2)   Such policies and procedures, including any reimbursement policies, are complied with by the person permitted thereunder to use the purchasing or procurement procedures described in this Article or established thereunder.

(c)   A violation of this section is a Class 1 misdemeanor.

§ 133-1. Employment of architects, etc., on public works when interested in use of materials prohibited.

It shall be unlawful for any architect, engineer, or other individual, firm, or corporation providing design services for any city, county or State work supported wholly or in part with public funds, knowingly to specify any building materials, equipment or other items which are manufactured, sold or distributed by any firm or corporation in which such designer or specifier has a financial interest by reason of being a partner, officer, employee, agent or substantial stockholder.

§ 133-2. Drawing of plans by material furnisher prohibited.

It shall be unlawful for any architect, engineer, designer or draftsman, employed on county, State, or city works, to employ or allow any manufacturer, his representatives or agents, to write, plan, draw, or make specifications for such works or any part thereof.

E. Related Statutory Provisions

§ 159-28. Budgetary accounting for appropriations.

(a)   Incurring Obligations. – No obligation may be incurred in a program, function, or activity accounted for in a fund included in the budget ordinance unless the budget ordinance includes an appropriation authorizing the obligation and an unencumbered balance remains in the appropriation sufficient to pay in the current fiscal year the sums obligated by the transaction for the current fiscal year. No obligation may be incurred for a capital project or a grant project authorized by a project ordinance unless that project ordinance includes an appropriation authorizing the obligation and an unencumbered balance remains in the appropriation sufficient to pay the sums obligated by the transaction. If an obligation is evidenced by a contract or agreement requiring the payment of money or by a purchase order for supplies and materials, the contract, agreement, or purchase order shall include on its face a certificate stating that the instrument has been preaudited to assure compliance with this subsection unless the obligation or a document related to the obligation has been approved by the Local Government Commission, in which case no certificate shall be required. The certificate, which shall be signed by the finance officer or any deputy finance officer approved for this purpose by the governing board, shall take substantially the following form:

"This instrument has been preaudited in the manner required by the Local Government Budget and Fiscal Control Act.

_____

(Signature of finance officer)."

Certificates in the form prescribed by G.S. 153-130 or 160-411 as those sections read on June 30, 1973, or by G.S. 159-28(b) as that section read on June 30, 1975, are sufficient until supplies of forms in existence on June 30, 1975, are exhausted.

An obligation incurred in violation of this subsection is invalid and may not be enforced. The finance officer shall establish procedures to assure compliance with this subsection.

(b)   Disbursements. – When a bill, invoice, or other claim against a local government or public authority is presented, the finance officer shall either approve or disapprove the necessary disbursement. If the claim involves a program, function, or activity accounted for in a fund included in the budget ordinance or a capital project or a grant project authorized by a project ordinance, the finance officer may approve the claim only if

    (1)   He determines the amount to be payable and

    (2)   The budget ordinance or a project ordinance includes an appropriation authorizing the expenditure and either (i) an encumbrance has been previously created for the transaction or (ii) an unencumbered balance remains in the appropriation sufficient to pay the amount to be disbursed.

The finance officer may approve a bill, invoice, or other claim requiring disbursement from an intragovernmental service fund or trust or agency fund not included in the budget ordinance, only if the amount claimed is determined to be payable. A bill, invoice, or other claim may not be paid unless it has been approved by the finance officer or, under subsection (c) of this section, by the governing board. The finance officer shall establish procedures to assure compliance with this subsection.

    (c)   Governing Board Approval of Bills, Invoices, or Claims. – The governing board may, as permitted by this subsection, approve a bill, invoice, or other claim against the local government or public authority that has been disapproved by the finance officer. It may not approve a claim for which no appropriation appears in the budget ordinance or in a project ordinance, or for which the appropriation contains no encumbrance and the unencumbered balance is less than the amount to be paid. The governing board shall approve payment by formal resolution stating the board's reasons for allowing the bill, invoice, or other claim. The resolution shall be entered in the minutes together with the names of those voting in the affirmative. The chairman of the board or some other member designated for this purpose shall sign the certificate on the check or draft given in payment of the bill, invoice, or other claim. If payment results in a violation of law, each member of the board voting to allow payment is jointly and severally liable for the full amount of the check or draft given in payment.

    (d)   Payment. – A local government or public authority may not pay a bill, invoice, salary, or other claim except by a check or draft on an official depository, a bank wire transfer from an official depository, or an electronic payment or an electronic funds transfer originated by the local government or public authority through an official depository. Except as provided in this subsection each check or draft on an official depository shall bear on its face a certificate signed by the finance officer or a deputy finance officer approved for this purpose by the governing board (or signed by the chairman or some other member of the board pursuant to subsection (c) of this section). The certificate shall take substantially the following form:

"This disbursement has been approved as required by the Local Government Budget and Fiscal Control Act.

_____

(Signature of finance officer)."

An electronic payment or electronic funds transfer must be subjected to the preaudit process. Execution of the electronic payment or electronic funds transfer shall indicate that the finance officer or duly appointed deputy finance officer has performed the preaudit process as required by G.S. 159-28(a).

Certificates in the form prescribed by G.S. 153-131 or 160-411.1 as those sections read on June 30, 1973, or by G.S. 159-28(a) as that section read on June 30, 1975, are sufficient until supplies in existence on June 30, 1975, are exhausted.

No certificate is required on payroll checks or drafts on an imprest account in an official depository, if the check or draft depositing the funds in the imprest account carried a signed certificate.

As used in this subsection, the term "electronic payment" means payment by charge card, credit card, debit card, or by electronic funds transfer, and the term "electronic funds transfer" means a transfer of funds initiated by using an electronic terminal, a telephone, a computer, or magnetic tape to instruct or authorize a financial institution or its agent to credit or debit an account.

(e) Penalties. – If an officer or employee of a local government or public authority incurs an obligation or pays out or causes to be paid out any funds in violation of this section, he and the sureties on his official bond are liable for any sums so committed or disbursed. If the finance officer or any properly designated deputy finance officer gives a false certificate to any contract, agreement, purchase order, check, draft, or other document, he and the sureties on his official bond are liable for any sums illegally committed or disbursed thereby.

§ 160A-20. Security interests.

(a)   Purchase. – A unit of local government may purchase, or finance or refinance the purchase of, real or personal property by installment contracts that create in some or all of the property purchased a security interest to secure payment of the purchase price to the seller or to an individual or entity advancing moneys or supplying financing for the purchase transaction.

(b)   Improvements. – A unit of local government may finance or refinance the construction or repair of fixtures or improvements on real property by contracts that create in some or all of the fixtures or improvements, or in all or some portion of the property on which the fixtures or improvements are located, or in both, a security interest to secure repayment of moneys advanced or made available for the construction or repair.

(c)   Accounts. – A unit of local government may use escrow accounts in connection with the advance funding of transactions authorized by this section, whereby the proceeds of the advance funding are invested pending disbursement. A unit of local government may also use other accounts, such as debt service payment accounts and debt service reserve accounts, to facilitate transactions authorized by this section. To secure transactions authorized by this section, a unit of local government may also create security interests in these accounts.

(d)   Nonsubstitution. – No contract entered into under this section may contain a nonsubstitution clause that restricts the right of a unit of local government to:

(1)   Continue to provide a service or activity; or

(2)   Replace or provide a substitute for any fixture, improvement, project, or property financed, refinanced, or purchased pursuant to the contract.

(e)   Oversight. – A contract entered into under this section is subject to approval by the Local Government Commission under Article 8 of Chapter 159 of the General Statutes if it:

(1)   Meets the standards set out in G.S. 159-148(a)(1), 159-148(a)(2), and 159-148(a)(3), or involves the construction or repair of fixtures or improvements on real property; and

(2)   Is not exempted from the provisions of that Article by one of the exemptions contained in G.S. 159-148(b).

(e1)   Public Hospitals. – A nonprofit entity operating or leasing a public hospital may enter into a contract pursuant to this section only if the nonprofit entity will have an ownership interest in the property being financed or refinanced, including a leasehold interest. The security interest granted in the property shall be only to the extent of the nonprofit entity's property interest. In addition, any contract entered into by a nonprofit entity operating or leasing a public hospital pursuant to this section is subject to the approval of the city, county, hospital district, or hospital authority that owns the hospital. Approval of the city, county, hospital district, or hospital authority may be withheld only under one or more of the following circumstances:

    (1)   The contract would cause the city, county, hospital district, or hospital authority to breach or violate any covenant in an existing financing instrument entered into by the nonprofit entity.

    (2)   The contract would restrict the ability of the city, county, hospital district, or hospital authority to incur anticipated bank-eligible indebtedness under federal tax laws.

    (3)   The entering into of the contract would have a material, adverse impact on the credit ratings of the city, county, hospital district, or hospital authority or would otherwise materially interfere with an anticipated financing by the nonprofit entity.

    (f)   Limit of Security. – No deficiency judgment may be rendered against any unit of local government in any action for breach of a contractual obligation authorized by this section. The taxing power of a unit of local government is not and may not be pledged directly or indirectly to secure any moneys due under a contract authorized by this section.

    (g)   Public Hearing. – Before entering into a contract under this section involving real property, a unit of local government shall hold a public hearing on the contract. A notice of the public hearing shall be published once at least 10 days before the date fixed for the hearing.

    (h)   Local Government Defined. – As used in this section, the term "unit of local government" means any of the following:

    (1)   A county.

    (2)   A city.

    (3)   A water and sewer authority created under Article 1 of Chapter 162A of the General Statutes.

    (3a)   A metropolitan sewerage district created under Article 5 of Chapter 162A of the General Statutes.

(3b) A sanitary district created under Part 2 of Article 2 of Chapter 130A of the General Statutes.

(3c) A county water and sewer district created under Article 6 of Chapter 162A of the General Statutes.

(4) An airport authority whose situs is entirely within a county that has (i) a population of over 120,000 according to the most recent federal decennial census and (ii) an area of less than 200 square miles.

(5) An airport authority in a county in which there are two incorporated municipalities with a population of more than 65,000 according to the most recent federal decennial census.

(5a) An airport board or commission authorized by agreement between two cities pursuant to G.S. 63-56, one of which is located partially but not wholly in the county in which the jointly owned airport is located, and where the board or commission provided water and wastewater services off the airport premises before January 1, 1995, except that the authority granted by this subdivision may be exercised by such a board or commission with respect to water and wastewater systems or improvements only.

(5b) A local airport authority that was created pursuant to a local act of the General Assembly.

(6) A local school administrative unit whose board of education is authorized to levy a school tax.

(6a) Any other local school administrative unit, but only for the purpose of financing energy conservation measures acquired pursuant to Part 2 of Article 3B of Chapter 143 of the General Statutes.

(6b) A community college, but only for the purpose of financing energy conservation measures acquired pursuant to Part 2 of Article 3B of Chapter 143 of the General Statutes.

(7) An area mental health, developmental disabilities, and substance abuse authority, acting in accordance with G.S. 122C-147.

(8) A consolidated citycounty, as defined by G.S. 160B-2(1).

(9) Repealed by Session Laws 2001-414, s. 52, effective September 14, 2001.

(10) A regional natural gas district, as defined by Article 28 of this Chapter.

(11) A regional public transportation authority or a regional transportation authority created pursuant to Article 26 or Article 27 of this Chapter.

(12) A nonprofit corporation or association operating or leasing a public hospital as defined in G.S. 159-39.

(13) A public health authority created under Part 1B of Article 2 of Chapter 130A of the General Statutes.

(14) A special district created under Article 43 of Chapter 105 of the General Statutes.

§ 115C-528. Lease purchase and installment purchase contracts for certain equipment.

(a) Local boards of education may purchase or finance the purchase of automobiles; school buses; mobile classroom units; food service equipment, photocopiers; and computers, computer hardware, computer software, and related support services by lease purchase contracts and installment purchase contracts as provided in this section. Computers, computer hardware, computer software, and related support services purchased under this section shall meet the technical standards specified in the North Carolina Instructional Technology Plan as developed and approved under G.S. 115C-102.6A and G.S. 115C-102.6B.

(b) A lease purchase contract under this section creates in the local board the right to possess and use the property for a specified period of time in exchange for periodic payments and shall include either an obligation or an option to purchase the property during the term of the contract. The contract may include an option to upgrade the property during the term. A local board may exercise an option to upgrade without rebidding the contract.

(c) An installment purchase contract under this section creates in the property purchased a security interest to secure payment of the purchase price to the seller or to an individual or entity advancing moneys or supplying financing for the purchase transaction.

(d) The term of a contract entered into under this section shall not exceed the useful life of the property purchased. An option to upgrade shall be considered in determining the useful life of the property.

(e) A contract entered into under this section shall be considered a continuing contract for capital outlay and subject to G.S. 115C-441(c1).

(f) A contract entered into under this section is subject to Article 8 of Chapter 159 of the General Statutes, except for G.S. 159-148(a)(4) and (b)(2). For purposes of determining whether the standards set out in G.S. 159-148(a)(3) have been met, only the five hundred thousand dollar ($500,000) threshold shall apply.

(g) Subsections (e) and (f) of this section shall not apply to contracts entered into under this section so long as the term of each contract does not exceed three years and the total amount financed during any three-year period is no greater than two hundred fifty thousand dollars ($250,000) or is no greater than three times the local board's annual State allocation for classroom materials, equipment, and instructional supplies, whichever is less. The local board shall submit information, including the principal and interest paid and the amount of outstanding obligation, concerning these contracts as part of the annual budget it submits to its board of county commissioners under Article 31 of this Chapter.

(h) No contract entered into under this section may contain a non-substitution clause that restricts the right of a local board to:

(1) Continue to provide a service or activity; or

(2) Replace or provide a substitute for any property financed or purchased by the contract.

(i) No deficiency judgment may be rendered against any local board of education or any unit of local government, as defined in G.S. 160A-20(h), in any action for breach of a contractual obligation authorized by this section, and the taxing power of a unit of local government is not and may not be pledged directly or indirectly to secure any moneys due under a contract authorized by this section.

§ 160A-17. Continuing contracts.

A city is authorized to enter into continuing contracts, some portion or all of which are to be performed in ensuing fiscal years. Sufficient funds shall be appropriated to meet any amount to be paid under the contract in the fiscal year in which it is made, and in each ensuing fiscal year, the council shall appropriate sufficient funds to meet the amounts to be paid during the fiscal year under continuing contracts previously entered into.

§ 153A-13. Continuing contracts.

A county may enter into continuing contracts, some portion or all of which are to be performed in ensuing fiscal years. In order to enter into such a contract, the county must have sufficient funds appropriated to meet any amount to be paid under the contract in the fiscal year in which it is made. In each year, the board of commissioners shall appropriate sufficient funds to meet the amounts to be paid during the fiscal year under continuing contracts previously entered into.

§ 160A-20.1. Contracts with private entities; contractors must use E-Verify.

(a)   Authority. – A city may contract with and appropriate money to any person, association, or corporation, in order to carry out any public purpose that the city is authorized by law to engage in. A city may not require a private contractor under this section to abide by any restriction that the city could not impose on all employers in the city, such as paying minimum wage or providing paid sick leave to its employees, as a condition of bidding on a contract.

(b)   Contractors Must Use E-Verify. – No city may enter into a contract subject to G.S. 143-129 unless the contractor and the contractor's subcontractors comply with the requirements of Article 2 of Chapter 64 of the General Statutes.

§ 153A-449. Contracts with private entities; contractors must use E-Verify.

(a)   Authority. – A county may contract with and appropriate money to any person, association, or corporation, in order to carry out any public purpose that the county is authorized by law to engage in. A county may not require a private contractor under this section to abide by any restriction that the county could not impose on all employers in the county, such as paying minimum wage or providing paid sick leave to its employees, as a condition of bidding on a contract.

(b)   Contractors Must Use E-Verify. – No county may enter into a contract subject to G.S. 143-129 unless the contractor and the contractor's subcontractors comply with the requirements of Article 2 of Chapter 64 of the General Statutes.

§ 160A-16. Contracts to be in writing; exception.

All contracts made by or on behalf of a city shall be in writing. A contract made in violation of this section shall be void and unenforceable unless it is expressly ratified by the council.

§ 25-2-201. Formal requirements; statute of frauds.

(1) Except as otherwise provided in this section a contract for the sale of goods for the price of five hundred dollars ($500.00) or more is not enforceable by way of action or defense unless there is some writing sufficient to indicate that a contract for sale has been made between the parties and signed by the party against whom enforcement is sought or by his authorized agent or broker. A writing is not insufficient because it omits or incorrectly states a term agreed upon but the contract is not enforceable under this paragraph beyond the quantity of goods shown in such writing.

(2) Between merchants if within a reasonable time a writing in confirmation of the contract and sufficient against the sender is received and the party receiving it has reason to know its contents, it satisfies the requirements of subsection (1) against such party unless written notice of objection to its contents is given within ten days after it is received.

(3) A contract which does not satisfy the requirements of subsection (1) but which is valid in other respects is enforceable

    (a) if the goods are to be specially manufactured for the buyer and are not suitable for sale to others in the ordinary course of the seller's business and the seller, before notice of repudiation is received and under circumstances which reasonably indicate that the goods are for the buyer, has made either a substantial beginning of their manufacture or commitments for their procurement; or

    (b) if the party against whom enforcement is sought admits in his pleading, testimony or otherwise in court that a contract for sale was made, but the contract is not enforceable under this provision beyond the quantity of goods admitted; or

(c) with respect to goods for which payment has been made and accepted or which have been received and accepted.

§ 22B-1. Construction indemnity agreements invalid.

Any promise or agreement in, or in connection with, a contract or agreement relative to the design, planning, construction, alteration, repair or maintenance of a building, structure, highway, road, appurtenance or appliance, including moving, demolition and excavating connected therewith, purporting to indemnify or hold harmless the promisee, the promisee's independent contractors, agents, employees, or indemnitees against liability for damages arising out of bodily injury to persons or damage to property proximately caused by or resulting from the negligence, in whole or in part, of the promisee, its independent contractors, agents, employees, or indemnitees, is against public policy and is void and unenforceable. Nothing contained in this section shall prevent or prohibit a contract, promise or agreement whereby a promisor shall indemnify or hold harmless any promisee or the promisee's independent contractors, agents, employees or indemnitees against liability for damages resulting from the sole negligence of the promisor, its agents or employees. This section shall not affect an insurance contract, workers' compensation, or any other agreement issued by an insurer, nor shall this section apply to promises or agreements under which a public utility as defined in G.S. 62-3(23) including a railroad corporation as an indemnitee. This section shall not apply to contracts entered into by the Department of Transportation pursuant to G.S. 136-28.1.

§ 22B-2. Contracts to improve real property.

A provision in any contract, subcontract, or purchase order for the improvement of real property in this State, or the providing of materials therefor, is void and against public policy if it makes the contract, subcontract, or purchase order subject to the laws of another state, or provides that the exclusive forum for any litigation, arbitration, or other dispute resolution process is located in another state.

§ 22B-3. Contracts with forum selection provisions.

Except as otherwise provided in this section, any provision in a contract entered into in North Carolina that requires the prosecution of any action or the arbitration of any dispute that arises from the contract to be instituted or heard in another state is against public policy and is void and unenforceable. This prohibition shall not apply to nonconsumer loan transactions or to any action or arbitration of a dispute that is commenced in another state pursuant to a forum selection provision with the consent of all parties to the contract at the time that the dispute arises.

§ 22B-10. Contract provisions waiving jury trial unenforceable.

Any provision in a contract requiring a party to the contract to waive his right to a jury trial is unconscionable as a matter of law and the provision shall be unenforceable. This section does not prohibit parties from entering into agreements to arbitrate or engage in other forms of alternative dispute resolution.

§ 143-134.3. No damage for delay clause.

No contractual language forbidding or limiting compensable damages for delays caused solely by the owner or its agent may be enforced in any construction contract let by any board or governing body of the State, or of any institution of State government, or of any county, city, town, or other political subdivision thereof. For purposes of this section, the phrase "owner or its agent" does not include prime contractors or their subcontractors.

§ 143-133.5. Public contracts; labor organizations.

(a)   It is the intent of the General Assembly that the provisions of this section will provide for more economical, nondiscriminatory, neutral, and efficient procurement of construction-related services by the State and political subdivisions of the State as market participants. The General Assembly finds that providing for fair and open competition best effectuates this intent.

(b)   Every officer, board, department, commission, or commissions charged with the responsibility of preparation of specifications or awarding or entering into contracts for the erection, construction, alteration, or repair of any buildings for the State, or for any county, municipality, or other public body subject to this Article shall not in any bid specifications, project agreements, or other controlling documents:

    (1)   Require or prohibit a bidder, offeror, contractor, or subcontractor from adhering to an agreement with one or more labor organizations in regard to that project or a related construction project.

    (2)   Otherwise discriminate against a bidder, offeror, contractor, or subcontractor for becoming, remaining, refusing to become or remain a signatory to, or for adhering or refusing to adhere to an agreement with one or more labor organizations in regard to that project or a related construction project.

(c)   No officer, board, department, commission, or commissions charged with the responsibility of awarding grants or tax incentives, or any county, municipality, or other public body in the award of grants or tax incentives, may award a grant or tax incentive that is conditioned upon a requirement that the awardee include a term described in subsection (b) of this section in a contract document for any construction, improvement, maintenance, or renovation to real property or fixtures that are the subject of the grant or tax incentive.

(d)   This section does not prohibit any officer, board, department, commission, or commissions or any county, municipality, or other public body from awarding a contract, grant, or tax incentive to a private owner, bidder, contractor, or subcontractor who enters into or who is party to an agreement with a labor organization if being or becoming a party or adhering to an agreement with a labor organization is not a condition for award of the contract, grant, or tax incentive, and if the State agent, employee, or board or the political subdivision does not discriminate against a private owner, bidder, contractor, or subcontractor in the awarding of that contract, grant, or tax incentive based upon the person's status as being or becoming, or the willingness or refusal to become, a party to an agreement with a labor organization.

(e)   This section does not prohibit a contractor or subcontractor from voluntarily entering into or complying with an agreement entered into with one or more labor organizations in regard to a contract with the State or a political subdivision of the State or funded in whole or in part from a grant or tax incentive from the State or political subdivision.

(f)   The State or the governing body of a political subdivision may exempt a particular project, contract, subcontract, grant, or tax incentive from the requirements of any or all of the provisions of subsection (b) or (c) of this section if the State or governing body of the political subdivision finds, after public notice and a hearing, that special circumstances require an exemption to avert a significant, documentable threat to public health or safety. A finding of special circumstances under this section shall not be based on the possibility or presence of a labor dispute concerning the use of contractors or subcontractors who are nonsignatories to, or otherwise do not adhere to, agreements with one or more labor organizations, or concerning employees on the project who are not members of or affiliated with a labor organization.

(g)   This section does not do either of the following:

   (1)   Prohibit employers or other parties from entering into agreements or engaging in any other activity protected by the National Labor Relations Act, 29 U.S.C. §§ 151 to 169.

   (2)   Interfere with labor relations of parties that are left unregulated under the National Labor Relations Act, 29 U.S.C. §§ 151 to 169.

www.ingramcontent.com/pod-product-compliance
Lightning Source LLC
Chambersburg PA
CBHW050526270326
41926CB00015B/3094